Best PUB WALKS in CORNWALL

Laurence Main

Copyright © L. Main, 1993

All Rights Reserved. No part of this publication may be reproduced, stored in a retrieval system, or transmitted in any form or by any means — electronic, mechanical, photocopying, recording, or otherwise — without prior written permission from the publisher.

Published by Sigma Leisure — an imprint of
Sigma Press, 1 South Oak Lane, Wilmslow, Cheshire SK9 6AR, England.

Reprinted 1996

British Library Cataloguing in Publication Data
A CIP record for this book is available from the British Library.

ISBN: 1-85058-306-4

Typesetting and design by: Sigma Press, Wilmslow, Cheshire.

Maps by: Morag Perrott

Text photographs by: Laurence Main

Cover photograph: THE PANDORA INN, RESTRONGUET. With kind permission of St. Austell Brewery Company Limited, St. Austell, Cornwall.

Cover design: MFP Design & Print

Printed and bound by: MFP Design & Print, 0161-864-4540

General Disclaimer

Whilst every effort has been made to ensure that the information given in this book is correct, neither the publisher nor the author accept any responsibility for any inaccuracy.

PREFACE

Cornow, or Kernow, means 'horn-shaped land'. The English added 'Wealas', meaning foreigners, to give the modern name of Cornwall. The English may think of it as one of their counties, but the spirit and history of the land demand its recognition as a Celtic nation, like Wales or Brittany. Until the 17th century, the linguistic links between Wales, Cornwall and Brittany were strong. Today some Cornish people are reviving the language, while the cross of St Piran proudly flies at Celtic festivals, such as the Welsh National Eisteddfod. The English didn't defeat the Cornish in battle until 838, at Hingston Down, near Callington. The River Tamar was declared the national boundary in 936 when Athelstan, King of Wessex, drove the Cornish out of Exeter.

There may not be Cornish Nationalist M.P.s at Westminster today, as with Wales and Scotland, but there is a national spirit and identity. This is expressed in the feeling for King Arthur and the harking back to a Celtic Golden Age, when the rest of the continent was in darkness. Arthur may or may not have been born at Tintagel, but some of the great characters of that period certainly lived here. While English Victorians seized upon Cornish locations for places in Arthurian stories, which were probably more to do with Wales, Somerset, Gloucestershire and Scotland, and locals welcomed the tourists' money, there's very good reason to trace the story of Tristan and Isoude (Iseult) in Cornwall.

There is even older magic and mystery in this enchanted land. The Giants of Albion may have erected the ancient stone monuments which may be of great significance. They seem to converge on the peninsula, like the spirit paths which peoples throughout the world recognise.

There's plenty more to learn about this and the best journal on the subject just happens to be located in Cornwall – The Ley Hunter (the International Magazine of Leys and Earth Mysteries), 39 Alma Place, Penzance, Cornwall, TR18 2BX. There is also a local magazine on the same subjects, but confined to Cornwall. This is *Meyn Mamvro*, 51 Carn Bosavern, St Just, near Penzance, TR19 7QX.

Cornwall is too popular with tourists for its scenic roads and charming old villages to bear, so do your bit by not coming here by car. You will gain the freedom of a surprisingly good public transport system. Despite the length of the county, it is possible (I've done it) to base yourself at one end, at Penzance, say, and do all of the walks in this book as day trips by bus and train. It takes a bit of planning, but this is enjoyable. There are only buses to Bude (via Truro) on certain days, for instance, but you can go all the way on a Western National Explorer ticket (fantastic value at £4 for an adult in 1992). It helps to take the train for long trips, such as from Penzance to Calstock, via Plymouth. This need not cost a lot. British Rail offer a Seven Day Cornish Rover (at £25 in 1992 – less then £4 per day) or a Three in Seven Day Cornish Rover (at £15 in 1992 – only £5 per day). A Seven Day Western National Bus Rover (Key West) cost £19.80 in 1992, while a Three Day Key West Bus Rover cost £12.

Of course, you need not stay in one place. There's plenty of all types of accommodation (including inns) and you could string the locations of these walks together on a tour of the county. Whatever you do, timetables are essential. Fortunately, Cornwall County Council realises the importance of presenting them all in one book, easily and cheaply available to tourists, both from Tourist Information Centres and through the post from the Passenger Transport Unit, County Hall, Truro, Cornwall, TR1 3BJ, Tel: 01872 74282. Western National also publishes a series of local timetable booklets (from Western National Limited, 21a Pydar Street, Truro, Cornwall, TR1 2AY, Tel: 01872 40404).

Cornwall is expert at coping with tourists, including walkers, and there are plenty of Tourist Information Centres, such as at Station Road (near the harbour), Penzance. Ask for a complete list and tourist information by post from the Cornwall Tourist Board, 59 Lemon Street, Truro, Cornwall, Tel: 01872 74057.

Laurence Main

CONTENTS

Introduction   1

Long Distance Paths   5

Cornish Real Ale   8

Location Map   14

The Walks

Location	*Distance*	*Pub*	
1. Bude	6$^1/_2$ miles	The Globe	16
2. Boscastle	7 miles	The Wellington	20
3. Tintagel	7 miles	The Wharncliffe Arms	28
4. Padstow	7$^1/_2$ miles	The Golden Lion	37
5. Jamaica Inn and Brown Willy	9 miles	The Jamaica Inn	44
6. Bodmin	6$^1/_2$ miles	The Hole in the Wall	49
7. Lostwithiel	12 miles	The Globe	55
8. The Hurlers and the Cheesewring	5 miles	The Caradon	63

Location	Distance	Pub	
9. Calstock	$4^1/_2$ miles	The Tamar	69
10. Newquay	10 miles	The Central	72
11. Fowey	8 miles	The Ship	78
12. West Looe	$5^1/_2$ miles	The Jolly Sailor	85
13. Mount Edgcumbe	5 miles	The Edgcumbe Arms	89
14. St Agnes	5 miles	Railway Inn	96
15. Truro	8 miles	The Famous Old Globe	101
16. Mevagissey	7 miles	The Ship	107
17. St.Ives	8 miles	The Sloop	112
18. Redruth Breweries	$5^1/_2$ miles	Rose Cottage	118
19. Restronguet	5 miles	The Pandora	124
20. St. Just	5 miles	The Kings Arms	128
21. Madron	$6^1/_2$ miles	King William IV	135
22. St Michael's Mount	9 miles	Godolphin Arms	142
23. Land's End	6 miles	The First and Last	148
24. Mousehole	5 miles	The Ship	154
25. The Loe	8 miles	Fitzsimmons Arms	160
26. Frenchman's Creek	$7^1/_2$ miles	The New Inn	167
27. Lizard	$6^1/_2$ miles	Top House	173

Introduction

'Kernow' is the Cornish for Cornwall

Monuments from the New Stone Age are abundant in Cornwall. We don't know who built them or why, but we know that they exist. They typify the air of mystery which pervades this part of the Celtic fringe. Great megalithic chamber tombs or quoits stand as mute evidence (not so mute – I spent a night in Chun Quoit and heard a horn blast, which resounded from 12.45 am to 1.45 am BST!).

The Bronze Age brought the construction of stone circles, especially in West Penwith and on Bodmin Moor. There is a particularly rich concentration of standing stones near the tip of the peninsula. They are the subject of John Michell's fascinating book *The Old Stones of Land's End*. They provide 'the evidence necessary for determining, once and for all, whether it is true, as claimed in Alfred Watkin's *The Old Straight Track*, that megalithic monuments were originally laid out in a series of straight alignments'. Michell's work has been added to by Ian Cooke with his *Journey to the Stones*.

The Romans came this way only to build a fort at Nanstallon (Bodmin, Walk 6). Cornwall was very much on the fringe of their empire, while the tin and copper that had earlier attracted traders from the Mediterranean seems to have been of less importance, at least in the early centuries of Roman power, when the mines of northern Spain were more notable. When the Romans withdrew in 410, the British Kingdom of Dumnonia emerged in good shape with a sophisticated centre at Tintagel. The Devon and Somerset portions of Dumnonia were lost by 800, however, when the English reached the River Tamar. They didn't gain control of Cornwall until the 10th century, leaving the Normans to make the Cornish feel dominated and exploited. Geography was on Cornwall's side, bringing the benefits of remoteness to the local language and culture. An important independent feature was the way that the resurgent tin industry had its own Stannary Courts, Laws and other privileges. Medieval monarchs granted exemption from taxes and manorial services, in return for heavily taxing the tin at coinage towns (Liskeard, Bodmin, Lostwithiel, Truro and Helston).

The Industrial Revolution dotted the Cornish landscape with mine engine houses. Cornwall was the world's major producer of tin and copper in the late 18th and for most of the 19th centuries. Ports and railways were developed, then copper was discovered in Australia and Chile, followed by the finding of tin in Malaya and Bolivia. Cornwall couldn't compete with these rich, cheap, sources and many Cornish miners emigrated to use their skills abroad. China clay extraction and the quarrying of stone have persisted, but the new railways had by now brought Cornwall a new source of wealth – the tourists.

The Victorians came to see the pixies, to hear about the ancient giants and to visit the places that Tennyson, especially, told them were identified with King Arthur. Gilbert and Sullivan produced their opera *The Pirates of Penzance* (actually, the first draft was entitled *The Pirates of Redruth*) and soon everybody who could afford a ticket on the Great Western Railway was enjoying the mild climate and the wonderful scenery during their holidays.

The north coast could be described as rugged and bracing, whilst the south is gentle and has numerous drowned river valleys. The spine of the county is formed of granite, from West Penwith via minor outcrops such as Carn Brea to Bodmin Moor. Purple heather and yellow gorse bring colour, while the stone 'hedges' are ablaze with differently coloured flowers on their sheltered sides in the summer.

Bird-watchers flock to the coast, where St Agnes Head (Walk 14) is famous for its kittiwakes, along with fulmars and peregrines. Puffins have been made rare by oil pollution, while choughs are now extinct in Cornwall. The estuaries and salt-marshes are home to shelduck and sandpipers. Seals and dolphins may be spotted from the cliff-tops and whales are sometimes left stranded on Cornish beaches. A few Cornish rivers can still boast otters, especially where the banks are well-wooded.

Religion has often stirred the Cornish people. Stephen Hawker's famous ballad was sung at the time of the trial of Bishop Trelawny and six others in 1688. Earlier, the imposition of an English Prayer Book in 1549 caused rebellion (one wonders if the Cornish language would have survived if the Bible had been translated into Cornish at the same time as it was translated into Welsh, in 1588). John Wesley had enormous success here, preaching to thousands and inspiring the erection of many Methodist Chapels.

Artists and writers have also been inspired by this place. Daphne du Maurier set her novels here, as at Frenchman's Creek (Walk 26) and Jamaica Inn (Walk 5). Walk 11 (Fowey) passes the novelist's former home at Menabilly. North Cornwall was Sir John Betjeman's favourite area, while D H Lawrence wrote much of *Women in Love* at Zennor. St Agnes (Walk 14) is *Poldark* country, as imagined by Winston Graham. The Boscastle area was important in the life of Thomas Hardy, whose novel, *A Pair of Blue Eyes* describes the cliffs walked on the second route in this book. D.M. Thomas, the author of *The White Hotel*, was born and lives in Cornwall. Sir Arthur Quiller-Couch based *Troy Town* on Fowey (Walk 11), while Dylan Thomas, the author of *Under Milk Wood* may have been influenced by Mousehole (Walk 24), where he stayed with his wife Caitlin after their wedding in Penzance. Virginia Woolf spent her childhood holidays at St Ives, which is famous for its colony of artists (who frequent the Sloop Inn, at the start of Walk 17). Artists love the clear light that the changeable maritime climate brings.

Above all this is a land of legend, where the Celtic past lives on in the place-names and the spirit endures amongst the people. Sadly, there's no need to learn the Cornish language to speak to the locals now, but a knowledge of it (or, even, Welsh) will bring the names of places alive.

'*By Tre, Pol and Pen,*
Ye shall know Cornishmen'

Well, *tre* means farm, homestead or
village, *pol* means a pool or pond,
while *pen* is head. *Avon* means river,
bot or *bod* means home (as in *abode*).
Bre or *brea* is hill, while *carn* means
rock, making Carn Brea a rocky hill.
Some other words with their English
meanings are:

A Cretean labyrinth near Tintagel

Byghan, bean or vean	small, little
Car, caer, gaer	fort, camp
Chy, che, jy, ty	house, cottage
Coad, coat, cot, got	a wood
Ddu, du, thew	black, dark
Eglos	church
Venton, fenton	spring, well
Glas, glaze	grey, green or blue
Goon, gun, woon	heath, down
Gwartha, worth	upper
Gwyn, wen, widden	white, fair
Hal, hale	moor, heath
Hel, hayle, el	estuary, river mouth
Hen	old
Hyr, ear, ir	long
Kelly, col	grove, wood
Lan	sacred enclosure
Lys, liz, les	court
Men, mayn	stone
Meneth, mena	hill
Mur, mear, vear	great, big
Nant, nans, nance	valley
Noweth, newth	new
Pons, pont	bridge
Porth, port	harbour, cove
Treth, dreth, draeth	beach
Whel, wheal	mine

Long Distance Paths

Cornwall is famous for its section of the South West Way, or South West Coast Path. The whole route from Minehead (in Somerset) to Poole (in Dorset) is reckoned to be 594 miles long. Some 268 miles are in Cornwall, from Marsland Mouth on the north coast via Land's End to the western shore of Plymouth Sound. Much of the Coast Path is formed by routes walked by Coastguards. Opened officially in 1973, it provides a major physical challenge,. having an interesting gradient profile to make up for the lack of mountains. The Coast Path is unsurpassed in its beauty.

Three of the official National Trail Guides published by Aurum Press in association with the Countryside Commission and the Ordnance Survey are needed to cover the Coast Path in Cornwall. These are for the *South West Coast Path – Minehead to Padstow* by Roland Tarr, *South West Coast Path – Padstow to Falmouth* by John Macadam and *South West Coast Path – Falmouth to Exmouth* by Brian Le Messurier. There is an independent body working in co-operation with the Ramblers' Association to improve the Coast Path. This is the South West Way Association. For membership details and/or publications list, send an s.a.e. to the Membership Secretary, Mrs Mary Macleod, 1 Orchard Drive, Kingskerswell, Newton Abbot, Devon, TQ12 5DG. This Association produces an invaluable annual guide to the Path, with details of accommodation, ferries (which can be a problem out of season), public transport, maps and publications plus diversions from the official route.

Cornwall's own version of a 'Coast to Coast Path' is *'Forth an Syns'*, or Saints Way. This is a walk of about 26 miles between Padstow, on the northern coast, and Fowey, on the southern. There is an alternative branch in the south, however, forking west near

Ancient Cross on the Saints Way

On the Coast Path, east of Tintagel

Helman Tor to reach Fowey via Luxulyan. This gives a total mileage of about 37 miles. The name comes from the fact that the Celtic Saints walked between these two harbours, to avoid a dangerous sea journey past Land's End (and Lyonesse?) when travelling between Wales and Brittany in the fifth and sixth centuries. There is no actual Saint's Path, as with the ancient Ridgeway, for example. This is more a linking of parish paths within the corridor of land walked by the Saints. As such, the Way takes the long distance walker into the attractive but little-known areas of mid-Cornwall. The Saints Way was formally opened in 1986 and is waymarked with crosses. *The Saints Way 'Forth an Syns'* by Michael Gill is available from CRS Member Relations Dept, 105 Station Road, St Blazey, Par, Cornwall, PL24 2LZ, although a new edition may be published by Cornwall County Council (ask in local Tourist Information Centres).

There is one more recognised long distance path in Cornwall. The Tinners Way is an 18 mile route which tries to follow the ancient paths used to transport tin and copper from the rich mining area around St Just to the sheltered harbour at St Ives. As such, this route was used for about 4000 years between the Bronze Age and the 19th century. With the Cornish name of *'Forth an Stenoryon'*, the route seems to be a trifle undefined, although waymarked with an engine house symbol. Walk 17 in this book follows a waymarked Tinners Way into St Ives. This is not the route described in Ian Cooke's excellent guidebook to The *Tinners Way*, which is Guide Four in his 'Antiquities of West Cornwall' series, available from Ian Cooke at the Men-an-Tol Studio, Bosullow, Penzance, Cornwall.

Finally, this isn't a long distance path (yet – what a challenge for somebody!) but an excellent idea for one. Hamish Miller and Paul Broadhurst's book 'The Sun and the Serpent' describes the famous ley or dragon line from Mount's Bay right up through southern England to the Norfolk Coast via such places as Glastonbury Tor, Avebury and Bury St Edmunds. This was outlined earlier by John Michell in his 'New View Over Atlantis'. Miller and Broadhurst have added wandering Michael and Mary energy lines (male and female) which coil around the dead straight ley. It would be a marvellous walk tracing these through Cornwall (even Miller and Broadhurst have only done it by motor-car).

Cornish Real Ale

When Walter Hicks mortgaged his farm for £1500 in 1851, little did he know how successful his new business in St Austell would be. Local brewers were commonplace then, with 24 operating in Cornwall. Hicks' was the only one to survive and thrive as an independent brewery in the late 20th century. He was lucky in that St Austell was flourishing thanks to the china clay industry. Tin and copper mining declined in the late 19th century, but the 7000 men, women and children employed in the 'white gold' mining around St Austell were protected from the ensuing depression.

Initially registering as one of Cornwall's 63 maltsters, Walter Hicks was trading as a wine and spirit merchant too by 1861. In 1869, his 'steam brewery' was built and his local competitors (six maltsters and three wine and spirit merchants) were all put out of business. He was St Austell's first and only major brewer, however, in place at the right time to meet the needs of a boom town.

Expansion brought a move to a grand new building in 1893, recalled by the great historian A.L. Rowse in 'A Cornish Childhood' as producing

'that more exotic scent...of malt or hops or of I do not know what aromatic spices they used in brewing, which the west wind blew across our playing fields, enveloping the school in its warm, soft, sweet, drowsy, liquorous smell, that insinuated itself into the passages and corridors and classrooms, came in puffs in at the windows, lurked heavily about the lower quarters of the school – and, in short, so wound itself into my mind that often when I think of those school days the memory of the nostalgic smell is entwined with them.'

St Austell Brewery has remained a family business. Walter junior helped his father from 1890 until his death in a motorcycle accident at Helston in 1911. Father and son had only registered as a limited company the previous year, but it proved strong enough to survive the blow. Walter senior returned to run affairs at the age of 82. He was succeeded in 1916 by his married daughter, Hester Parnall. She dominated affairs till her death in 1939.

1939 also saw a disastrous fire, destroying all the garages, shops and stores, four lorries and the brewery records. Egbert Barnes, the son of Walter Hick's other daughter, Mary, steered the Brewery back to stability during the 40 years he was Chairman. The present incumbent is married to Walter Hicks' great-granddaughter. The family tradition is reflected in the company staff.

Beer has been the chief drink of England throughout its history. Local breweries, including those in monasteries and great estates, were common until the 18th century. When Walter Hicks' new 'steam brewery' was visited by a journalist from 'The West Briton' in 1870, he marvelled at its:

'four stories, the upper being fitted with three bins each capable of containing 100 bushels of malt, also two furnaces sufficiently large to hold 2000 and 1000 gallons. By a new and admirable apparatus the mashing is most successfully carried on. The next floor has two large receivers. After the beer has been boiled it is poured into these vessels in which it passes to the next flat and immediately falls on a patent refrigerator. This ingenious and useful appliance is made of a number of copper tubes perpendicularly set, through which cold water is constantly flowing, as soon as the beer drops off it is then passed at its required temperature into the vats which are quite in keeping with the other portions of the building. The brewery is well supplied with spring water which is pumped by a steam engine of 3 hp. The cellar is very capacious.'

Victorian technology not withstanding, this is very similar to the way beer was made in the medieval monasteries. The best of the past has been kept by this Brewery, with glossy wooden lagging and huge copper and brass lids on the cast iron mash tuns, alongside shiny modern stainless steel. There is one remaining original slate fermenting vessel made by Ernest Matthews & Co., Slate Back Manufacturers of London and Bristol.

St Austell still uses the traditional Tower System of brewing. The ingredients are taken to the top of the tower and progress between each stage in the brewing process with the aid of gravity. The first stage is milling. Malted barley, already softened by soaking to encourage germination, is broken down to make the grain more soluble. Only the best ingredients are used.

This milled malt, or grist, is mixed with water, or liquor, and heated to 165°F in the mash tuns on the next floor. Bubbling like hot porridge and smelling like biscuits, the mixture, known as 'the goods', is given an hour to stand in the tuns. This allows the liquor to change the character of the grist and yield a sugary, malty, solution, which is fermentable. The goods are then sprayed, or 'sparged', with hot liquor. This extracts the malty sugars and produces a solution known as 'raw wort'. This is honey-coloured and tastes of malt syrup. After all the wort has been separated from it, the spent grist is taken out and sold as cattle feed.

The wort descents to the copper, a huge cauldron. The hops are added to it here and the whole is boiled for nearly two hours. High quality hops are essential for a good flavour, so only the best are used here (Fuggles and Goldings). the 'hopped wort' is boiled to remove unwanted proteins, to sterilise it and to extract any bitterness from the hops. After 30 minutes resting in a 'hop back', where the hops settle to the bottom, the wort filters through the hops and proceeds to the cooling process. Nothing is wasted – the spent hops make a good fertiliser.

The next part of the process, cooling the wort, has been accelerated with the aid of modern technology. Yeast is added when the wort has been cooled from 215°F to 64°F. A modern type of 'patent refrigerator' can handle 3600 gallons (100 barrels) in an hour. The wort is then pumped to fermenting vessels, where the strength of the wort is checked for the benefit of both the Brewer and the Customs and Excise Officers, who now collect their Beer Duty. The wort and yeast remain in the twelve fermenting vessels for a week.

Cooling pipes maintain the temperature at about 67°F, to control the speed at which the yeast works. This living fungus is the magic ingredient of beer and gives the foaming head on the top of the wort. The yeast turns the wort's sugar into alcohol and carbon dioxide, whilst multiplying itself. The yeast is skimmed off after primary fermentation, pressed and kept in a cold store to be used again. Any excess yeast is sold to be fed to pigs.

Fermentation is a delicate stage in brewing, making it critical to the reputation of the Brewery. The fermenting vessels contain the beer for at least one week. Brewing is then complete.

Different beers can be produced by altering the quantity of liquor added and the degree to which the subsequent wort is fermented. The St Austell Brewery produces traditional cask-conditioned draught ale, as well as keg and bottle. A premium lager is also made.

Hicks Special Draught (HSD), Tinners, Bosuns and XXXX Mild are all traditional cask-conditioned draught beers. They are put into the casks from the fermenting vessels and have finings added (made from the swim bladder of the sturgeon) in order to give a clear pint, before they are distributed. A special dry hop flavour is given to Tinners and HSD by the addition of a small quantity of aromatic hops.

By contrast, Duchy and Wreckers are keg beers. These are left in a tank at a constant temperature of about 57°F for between a week and 10 days. During this time the remaining yeast ferments any residual sugars. The beer is then chilled and kept overnight at 32°F, before being filtered. This ensures the removal of any solids. The beer is pasteurised (sterilised) and kegged.

Light, Brown and Duchy are bottled beers, produced in the same way as keg beers. Beers in bottles with the Prince's and Smuggler's labels have been allowed to age in the cold tanks and gain distinctive characters. The premium lager, Export Gold, has a very different brewing process. Its malt has a pale colour, having been very lightly kilned. It is then fermented at a low temperature, with the yeast dropping to the bottom of the vessel. This avoids the frothy heads found with traditional ale. The word 'lager' refers to the long period that it is stored (several weeks). During this time it is kept at low temperature so that the remaining sugars are fermented out.

St Austell Brewery still employs a resident cooper and the old wooden casks can be seen in some pubs. Most barrels today are made of aluminium, of course, but the oak staves from disused casks are re-used and the Brewery has over 500 left in stock.

The essence of beer is its water. St Austell Brewery has its own supply from a spring. The water is clear and pure and comes from a deep, natural, reservoir.

St Austell Brewery has public houses all over Cornwall, many of them offering accommodation as well as real ale. The Brewery publishes an Inn Guide, a 'Kernow' Cornish Passport scheme with prizes for visiting set numbers of their pubs and welcomes visitors to their Brewery, during the holiday season. For more details of the inns providing hospitality, contact St Austell brewery, Trevarthian Road, St Austell, PL25 4BY (tel 01726 67970). To book a place on a brewery tour, telephone 01726 66022. The following pubs belong to the St Austell Brewery and are featured in this book: The Globe, Bude (Walk 1), The Central, Newquay (Walk 10), The Pandora, Restronguet (Walk 19), The Ship, Fowey (Walk 11), The Ship, Mevagissey (Walk 16), The Fire Engine, Marazion (Walk 22), The Ship, Mousehole (Walk 26) and The Kings Arms, St Just (Walk 20).

Opening Hours

Under recent legislation pubs in England can now open for a maximum of 12 hours each day on Mondays to Saturdays (being 11 am to 11 pm) and for six and a half hours on Sundays (noon to 3 pm and 7 pm to 10.30 pm) unless extensions have been granted by local licensing magistrates. Additionally, a growing number of pubs stay open during Sunday afternoons to serve meals, with which alcohol may then be consumed on the premises. Most country pubs do not find it in their interest to take full advantage of these 'relaxed' hours and tend to stick to the 'traditional' hours of noon to 3 pm and 6 pm to 11 pm or 7 pm to 11 pm. Check each pub individually.

The Walks

Each of the walks in this book follows rights of way to which you, as a member of the public, have unrestricted access. These are public footpaths, bridleways and by-ways as well as lanes and roads. When surveyed, all these routes were free of obstructions. Should you discover any problems on rights of way in Cornwall, send full details (including grid references) to the Ramblers' Association at 1/5 Wandsworth Road, London, SW8 2XX and contact the Footpaths Section, County Highways, Truro, tel 01872 74282.

The walks are numbered in sequence (almost) from north to south and are spread all over Cornwall. Make use of the Ordnance Survey Pathfinder Maps, details of which are given for each walk. These are beautiful keys to the countryside which all walkers should become familiar with.

All walks should be within the capabilities of anyone of average fitness. Allow about one hour for every two miles, which should enable short breaks to be made. Do not be surprised by the strenuous nature of Coast Path walking, which may involve a lot of climbing. Do remember that the physical landscape is changing all the time, for example as hedgerows are grubbed up and fields amalgamated. Keep to the path and always regard it as a privilege to walk across someone else's land; in that way we can build an atmosphere of co-operation, rather than confrontation, in the countryside.

The Country Code

❏ Guard against all risk of fire.

❏ Fasten all gates.

❏ Keep dogs under proper control.

❏ Avoid damaging fences, hedges and walls.

❏ Keep to paths across farmland.

❏ Leave no litter.

❏ Safeguard water supplies.

❏ Protect wildlife, wild plants and trees.

❏ Go carefully on country roads.

❏ Respect the life of the countryside.

LOCATION MAP

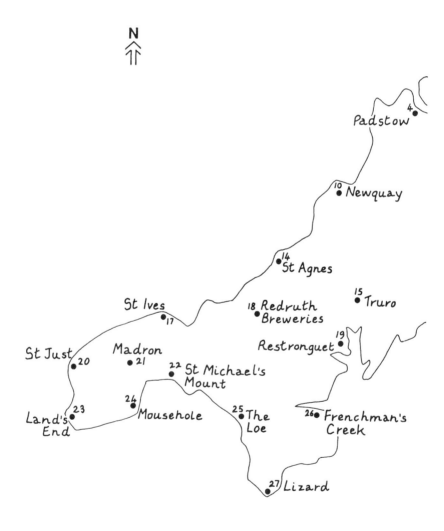

1. Bude

Route: Bude – Bude Canal – Helebridge – Coast Path – Bude.

Distance: $6^1/_2$ miles.

Map: O.S. Pathfinder 1292 Bude and Holsworthy

Start: The Globe, Bude (Grid Reference SS 209063)

Access: Buses run to Bude from all parts, including Truro (No. X3 via Launceston and No. X4 via Tintagel), Bideford (No. 85), Boscastle (No. 202), Exeter (No. 209), Plymouth (No. 221) and Tintagel (No. 239).

The Globe (01288 352085)

'Giant' Haystacks created a stir when he stayed here. The bar staff patiently explained to me that he is a famous wrestler. You can sup real ale, enjoy a meal or stay for a night or two on a bed and breakfast basis if you wish. Bar opening hours are 11 am to 11 pm on week-days, noon to 3 pm and 7 pm to 10.30 pm on Sundays.

Bude

Bude is a small family resort in the neglected north-east of Cornwall. This was border country, as the name of Whalesborough Farm indicates. Saxons settled here, on the very edge of Celtic territory. The London and South Western Railway finally arrived in 1898, as a branchline from the mainline at Halwill Junction, Southern Region's Atlantic Coast Express had its through carriage from London Waterloo detached here. The line was short-sightedly closed in 1966, leaving this part of Cornwall bereft of railways.

Two miles of the canal that once linked Bude and Launceston have survived since the 1920s, although the canal was abandoned in 1891. It was dug to carry sand from Bude Haven to the arable land of the interior. The sand was rich in calcium and made a good fertiliser, along with lime and seaweed. Coal from South Wales was also imported, while slate and grain were sent out. The canal had to negotiate a hilly interior, however, which would have called for a large number of conventional locks. The unique local answer was to use tub-boats. These were only 20 feet long by 5ft 6ins wide and were designed to be pulled in trains of four or five at a time by horses. When they came to the hills, they were hauled out and revealed wheels. These were used along railed tracks up inclines, worked by an ingenious use of water power. One such incline can be seen east of Helebridge, near Marhamchurch. The Museum near the end of this walk can provide more information on this.

Now Bude Marshes form a Nature Reserve, with herons, swans, mallards and moorhens. One place of note, just before Bude's museum, is a small castle built in 1850 by Sir Goldsworthy Gurney. He was an engineer who invented the Bude Light, an oxy-hydrogen limelight, used for lighthouses. He also found a way of building on sand and built his castle, once his home and now council offices, to prove it.

The Walk

1. Cross the road (The Strand) to the pavement opposite. Turn left to walk upstream with the River Neet on your right. Turn right across a bridge and pass a large car park on your left. Approach a second bridge.

2. Do not cross the second bridge. Turn left just before it, to follow the tow-path of the Bude Canal. Walk with the canal on your right. Pass a Nature Reserve on your left. Reach a minor road and turn right with it to cross the canal by a bridge. Turn left along the canal tow-path again, but with the canal on your left now.

3. Reach the A39 road. If you wish to divert to see the old canal incline near Marhamchurch, cross the road carefully and continue along the tow-path. Otherwise, go right beside the A39 and turn right very soon, opposite the road to Marhamchurch. Go ahead over a cattle grid and a flat bridge to follow a concrete access Lane.

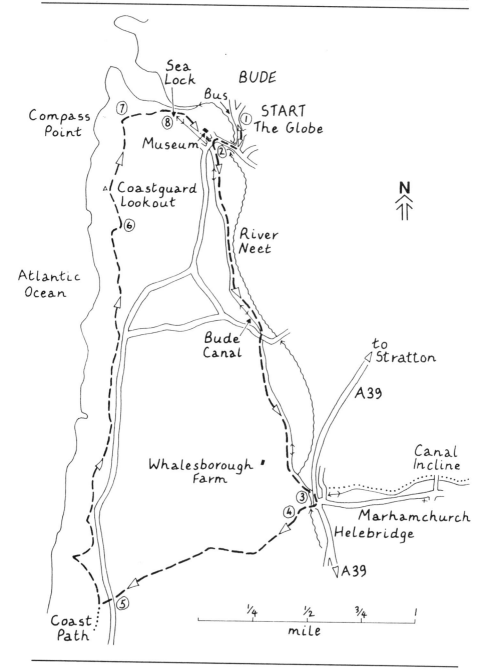

4. Turn left over a stile and follow the waymarked field-path. This bears right to cross the field diagonally. Go ahead over a waymarked stile in the corner and beside a hedge on your left in the next field. Continue along this waymarked route until you reach a road.

5. Go ahead across the road and towards the sea. Turn right along the Coast Path and walk above the sea on your left.

6. Bear left at a fork, to keep with the Coast Path. Reach Compass Point, with its spectacular views.

7. Turn right down to the canal's sea lock.

8. Cross to the far side of the canal at the lock. Turn right to walk inland with the canal on your right. Visit the museum on your left. Reach the road and go left to retrace your steps into Bude.

2. Boscastle

Route: Boscastle – Willapark – Trevalga – Trehane Farm – Boscastle – Pentargon – Boscastle.

Distance: 7 miles

Maps: O.S. Pathfinders 1325 Camelford (essential) plus 1310 St Gennys (you could get by without this one)

Start: The Wellington Hotel, Boscastle (Grid Reference SX 099912)

Access: Buses stop near the Wellington Hotel, Boscastle, from Truro (X4), Wadebridge (No. 52), Bude (Nos. X4 and 202), Plymouth (No. 241), Launceston (No. 230), Bodmin (Nos. X4 and 245) and Tintagel (Nos. X4, 52, 239, 240, 241, 245 and 202).

The Wellington Hotel (01840 250202)

'*The Welly*' is famous for its English and French food, served in its own Georgian Restaurant know as '*La Belle Alliance*'. Local lobster is usually on the menu. This 16th Century inn was called the Boscastle Hotel until the death of the 'Iron Duke' in 1852 prompted a change of name. Famous visitors have included Edward VII, when Prince of Wales, Thomas Hardy and Guy Gibson VC, of Dambusters fame. Real ale is served, while you are welcome to stay for bed and breakfast. Bar opening hours are 11 am to 3 pm and 5.30 pm to 11 pm on weekdays (till midnight on Mondays, when there is folk music), noon to 3 pm and 7 pm to 10.30 pm on Sundays.

The Napoleon Inn (01840 250204)

If Wellington's at the bottom of the hill, Napoleon is bound to be at the top! Actually, it's Boney's Bar and is named after William Bone, a former landlord who was sent to Bodmin Gaol in 1858 for soliciting and holding a house of ill-repute. Volunteers used to take the King's shilling here during the Napoleonic wars. Nowadays it is famous for its real ale, its

The Wellington Hotel

food (which has earned it a place in the Egon Roney Good Food Guide) and for being selected as one of the 12 best 'character' pubs of Great Britain by Teachers' Whisky in 1989. Opening hours are 11 am to 3 pm and 6 pm to 11 pm on weekdays, noon to 3 pm and 7 pm to 10.30 pm on Sundays.

Boscastle

Boscastle possesses the only natural harbour in 40 miles of coastline between Padstow and Hartland. This prompted Sir Richard Grenville to rebuild it in 1584. The port served as a place for fertiliser and lime to be imported for the interior, around Launceston, while slate and corn were exported. Wagons and packhorses were a regular feature of the scene here, with the horses being stabled in what is now the youth hostel (one of the Y.H.A.'s best). So isolated was Boscastle from the rest of the land (the nearest railway station in Camelford didn't open until 1893) that horse drawn coaches were still driven to the Wellington Hotel in the 1920s. This seemingly backward remoteness made it just the place for witches to live. Anybody visiting the Witchcraft Museum is left in no doubt of the reality of their existence, so come prepared with some garlic hanging around your neck!

When Thomas Hardy came here in March 1870, he was soon bewitched by Emma Gifford. He was the young architect engaged to restore the church at nearby St Juliot, while she was the young sister-in-law and housekeeper of the rector. They married in 1874, after his novel 'Far from the Madding Crowd' proved successful. Their marriage was not the happiest. Memories of their early happy times flooded back to Hardy after Emma's death in 1912, however. He returned here and wrote about them. The cliffs above Pentargon Bay were captured in the poem 'Beeny Cliff':

'O the opal and the sapphire of that wandering western sea,
And the woman riding high above with bright hair flapping free -
The woman whom I loved so, and who loyally loved me.
The pale mews plained below us, and the waves seemed far away.
In a nether sky, engrossed in saying their ceaseless babbling say,
As we laughed light-heartedly aloft on that clear-sunned March day ...'

Earlier, in his novel 'Pair of Blue Eyes' (1873), Elfride Swancourt could not *'bear to look at the cliff ... it has a horrid personality and makes me shudder'*. Her lover, Henry Knight, pursues his hat, goes too close to the edge of the cliff and slips dangerously. This cliff, above Pentargon, is vital to the plot. The waterfall that runs over the precipice as you turn towards the cliff, was one of the first places Hardy revisited after Emma's death. He imagines in 'After a Journey' that Emma leads him back there:

'I see what you are doing: you are leading me on
To the spots we knew when we haunted here together,
The waterfall, above which the mist bow shone
At the then fair hour in the then fair weather,
And the cave just under, with a voice still so hollow
That it seems to call out to me from forty years ago...'

Looking back in 1895, in his preface to 'A Pair of Blue Eyes', Hardy described the shore and country about Boscastle (Castle Boterel) as being a region *'of dream and mystery'*, that *'the ghostly birds, the pall-like sea, the frothy wind, the eternal soliloquy of the waters, the bloom of dark purple cast, that seems to exhale from the shoreward precipices, in themselves lend to the scene an atmosphere like the twilight of a night vision.'* Hardy's use of 'Castle Boterel' was a revival of the village's old name. The de Botterell family had followed William the Conqueror over from France and built Bottraeux Castle here.

The Walk

This figure of eight route could easily be split into two shorter walks from the Wellington Hotel, Boscastle.

1. Go right to the road junction and turn left uphill along the road to a hairpin bend. Go straight ahead, away from the road as it bends sharply left, along the Coast Path. If there is a lot of traffic, avoid this short stretch of road walking by taking the lower track, near the River Valency and climb to the Coast Path. Walk above the harbour on your right, towards Willapark Headland.

2. Follow the waymarked Coast Path as it bends left to pass the mouth of Boscastle Harbour on your right. The rocky island is Meachard. Fork right to the old Coastguard Station, where the views are excellent.

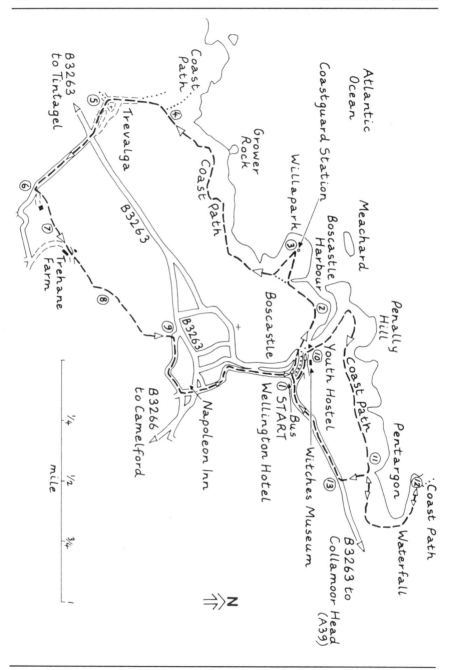

The old Coast Guard Station on Willapark, overlooking Boscastle Harbour

3. Descend to the Coast Path and go right, walking with the sea on your right. The Coast Path eventually becomes a rutted track. Come to a waymark post pointing towards Trevalga.

4. Ignore the Coast Path going right. Take the rutted track inland. Join the access lane from the Manor House and go left along it to the Church of St Petroc, Trevalga.

5. Continue along the rough lane to a No Through Road at a telephone box. Go right to the B3263 road. Cross carefully and go up the lane opposite. Pass an old chapel on your right.

6. Turn left along a track signposted as a Public Footpath. Fork left at a wooden signpost just before the track goes through a gate ahead. Follow the footpath past a hedge on your right. Emerge at a gate. Go ahead along the right hand edge of a field. When the wall on your right turns right, cut across the corner of the field ahead to the gate opposite.

7. Go ahead with a hedge on your right. Take the wooden gate into a farmyard and continue past the farm buildings to Trehane Farm on your right and the farmhouse on your left. Continue with the hedge on your right in the following field. Take the waymarked gap into the next field and bear left down to a waymark post in the corner.

8. Continue beside a hedge on your right and go over a slate stile in the next corner. Bear slightly left downhill to a stile (above a gate) in the next field. Continue down the following field to a stile just above its corner. Reach a rough track and go left down it to a road.

9. Do not go ahead to the B3263 road. Do turn right immediately to take the quiet road. Reach a crossroads and turn left downhill. Pass the Napoleon Inn on your left. Continue downhill, crossing the B3263 with care. Pass the Methodist Church on your right and the Junior School on your left. Follow the road as it bends left to pass the Post Office on your left. Fork right downhill to reach the Wellington Hotel on your right. NOW START THE SECOND LOOP OF THIS FIGURE OF EIGHT ROUTE. Go right, across the bridge over the Valency River. Turn left to pass the Witchcraft Museum on your right.

10. Fork right up the signposted Coast Path, passing the Pixie Shop on your left. Walk above the harbour on your left. Admire the view over

the sea and turn sharply right at a red box with 'cliff rope' marked on it. Keep inland and climb to a flagstaff. Bear right along the Coast Path above the sea on your left. Approach the sheer, black, cliffs of Pentargon Bay.

11. Turn right over a slate stile. Go left beside a wall on your left to a wooden stile. Turn left over it and continue with a wall on your left and uphill to a stile ahead. Cross it and walk beside a wall on your right. Reach a waymark post and descend steeply. Go up steps, zigzagging first left, then right, then left again. Cross a footbridge over a stream, then ascend as waymarked. Walk along the path with the bay on your left. Look for a view back towards the waterfall.

12. Retrace your steps down to the footbridge and up the other side, over a stile and on to the second, wooden, stile. Leave the Coast Path by turning left with the wall on your left. Go over a waymarked stile beside a gate ahead. Follow a wall on your left to the corner. Go through a kissing gate beside a gate to a road.

13. Turn right along the road. Follow it back to Boscastle or, if traffic is heavy, immediately after the drive to Pennally House, bear right through a white gate (a National Trust sign says 'Footpath to Boscastle Harbour'). This grassy track takes you back to the outward path at the Pixie Shop. Go left back to the Wellington Hotel.

3. Tintagel

Route: Tintagel – St Materiana's Church – Dunderhole Point – Coast Path – Tintagel Castle – Coast Path – Rocky Valley – St Piran's Well – St Nectan's Glen – Tintagel

Distance: 7 miles

Map: O.S. Pathfinder 1325 Camelford

Start: The Wharncliff Arms Hotel, Tintagel (Grid Reference SX 058884)

Access: There are several bus companies competing to Tintagel. This means that you must be careful before investing in return tickets (if available) or rover tickets. No. X4 between Truro and Bude is run by Western National, so you can use their Explorer and Key West Tickets on it. There are also Nos. 52 (between Boscastle and Wadebridge), 240 (from Launceston), 241 (from Plymouth), 245 (between Boscastle and Bodmin), 247 (from Wadebridge), 248 (from Camelford) and 239 (from Bude).

The Wharncliff Arms Hotel, Tintagel (01840 770393)

Real ale, food and accommodation are available at this hotel. The bar opening hours are 11.30 am to 3 pm and 6 pm to 11 pm on weekdays, noon to 2.30 pm and 7 pm to 10.30 pm on Sundays. The place is haunted by the ghost of a man who was kicked to death by a horse in the 19th century. Peter Cushing has stayed here, while Paul Daniels once called by to use the loo.

King Arthur's Arms (01840 770831)

Real ale, food and accommodation are available here too. Bar opening hours are 11 am to 11 pm on weekdays, noon to 3 pm and 7 pm to 10.30 pm on Sundays.

Tintagel

'But after tempest, when the long wave broke
All down the thundering shores of Bude and Bos,
There came a day as still as heaven, and then
They found a naked child upon the sands
Of dark Tintagel by the Cornish Sea;
And that was Arthur; and they foster'd him
Till he by miracle was approven King...'

It didn't happen quite like that, but Tennyson had to write for Victorians who didn't care for the old legend explaining Arthur's birth. This has King Uther (Victor) or Uther Pendragon (Head war-lord – these were titles, not personal names) falling in love with Ygerna, who happened to be the wife of Gorlois, the Duke of Cornwall (then part of Dumnonia).

Uther called all the notables of the realm to an Easter feast at which he made his feelings for Ygerna so obvious that her husband took her home early in a rage. Uther followed with an army but couldn't take the lady as she was on a virtual island, joined to the mainland by the narrowest of necks of land, that three men could defend easily. The place was called Tintagel because there was a fort (tin or din) and a tagell (narrow access). It was and is so nearly an island that this natural bridge (tourists now cross by an artificial bridge) has a cave running right through it. This is known as Merlin's Cave.

Uther was magically changed by Merlin to appear like Gorlois. He then gained access to Ygerna's bed-chamber, where Arthur was conceived. Gorlois was killed in battle, Ygerna became Uther's wife and Merlin took the baby to be fostered.

Tennyson's English readers may have swallowed his line, but then most people today think that Arthur was King of England, when the English were his enemies. Welsh records make it clear who Arthur was. Born about 500 (to allow for the Celtic Church counting its years from the

'The Island', Tintagel

crucifixion in 37 AD) and being mortally wounded about 574 (i.e. the 537 of Welsh annals plus 37), Arthur was the son of Meurig, son of Tewdrig. His kingdom was Ancient Siluria, based on what is now Gwent and Glamorgan, but extending to Gloucestershire, Avon and part of Somerset. He was known as Arthur Machen, a place which still exists on the Gwent/Glamorgan border, as does Cerniw, so easily confused with Cornwall (which was part of Dumnonia in Arthurian times).

The mythical Arthur was also a composite character, with an ancestor of the sixth century Arthur, also called Arthur, fighting with the Roman Emperor Magnus Maximus (Macsen Wledig). Similarly, in a thousand years time it might be easy to confuse the Churchill who was rewarded for his victories in the 18th century over the French by the gift of Blenheim Palace with the Churchill who was later born there and fought the Germans in the 20th century.

This doesn't rule out the possibility that King Arthur was born at Tintagel. After all, the local church was reputedly founded by St Materiana, who came from Gwent around 500.

Geoffrey of Monmouth, who wrote his 'History of the Kings of Britain' at Oxford in about 1140 and knew the Welsh legends, whilst being inspired, he said, by an ancient book from Brittany, must have had some reason to specify Tintagel. He is know to have visited here in 1134.

Recent excavations have shown that a rich community did live here in Arthurian times, importing wine and olive oil from places like Antioch and Alexandria (probably in exchange for Cornish tin). What's more, the churchyard has revealed fifth and sixth century mound graves of prominent, Christian, people. There can be no doubt that Tintagel was the local place of importance at that time.

But there is much more than these dry bones to consider. The very air here is full of magic. We have to think on a different plane. Forget the historical Arthur (who most certainly did exist) and consider the symbolic Once and Future King. This is the spot where a druid would cause him to be incarnated. It is the message behind the legend that counts. Psychics have a field day here and theories abound. The sum of them all is that this is an especially magical spot. It has attracted the likes of Turner, who painted it in 1819, Tennyson, who wrote his poem 'Morte d'Arthur' in 1842 and returned to gain inspiration for 'The Idylls of the King', Charles Dickens and the poet Algernon Swinburne.

This significant site has a fame rooted in an ancient understanding that has been lost as we have moved away from Nature. Symbolic riddles are now taken to be fanciful notions. As we are forced to return to the ancient understanding, Tintagel and its kind loom in our consciousness, restoring the spiritual link with the Living Earth and with Arthur, the heroic protector of Britain, who can be relied upon in our hour of need.

The symbolic value was recognised by Richard, the younger brother of King Henry III, who was created Earl of Cornwall in 1227 and styled himself King of the Romans. It is his castle's ruins that the tourists wander through. Now in the care of English Heritage, it is open daily from April to September between 10 am and 6 pm. From October to March, it is open between Tuesdays and Sundays, from 10 am to 4 pm (closed from 24th to 26th December and on 1st January).

Many visitors are put off by their first impression of the village of Tintagel. It is over-commercialised and has exploited the Arthurian connection to the hilt. It would have been better if it had retained its

Tintagel Castle

former name of Trevena (just one settlement within the parish of Tintagel). Perhaps it is fitting, however, that the real Tintagel can only be experienced by those who are prepared to walk (one fit, young, lady who had come all the way from Germany stood at the top of the steps when I was there and decided that the steep descent and ascent wasn't worth it!). When the North Cornwall Railway reached Camelford in 1893, it was soon followed by the construction of Arthur's Castle Hotel. This prompted the National Trust to save the nearby cliffs by buying 14 acres of Barras Nose, their first coastal property in England, in 1897. King Arthur's Halls, next to the start of this walk, were built between 1929 and 1933 by Mr Frederick Glasscock, a millionaire jelly and custard powder maker, who chose to retire here. The exhibition is open daily from Easter to October (Tel. 01840 770526) and you can browse in the bookstall for free.

Do visit the Old Post Office before leaving Tintagel. This was used by the Post Office between 1844 and 1892, but it is also a fine example of a yeoman's house of about 1400. In the care of the National Trust, who bought it in 1903, it is open from April to October between 11 am and 6 pm (5 pm in October).

The church is isolated and ancient. The dedication to St Materiana is suspiciously like one to the Mother Goddess. It houses a Roman milestone from the time of the emperor Licinius (308 – 324 AD). One touching grave outside is of Domenico Catanese, the ship's boy from the wrecked barque 'Iota'. She was lost on Lye Rock in a blizzard in December, 1893, taking coal from Cardiff to Trinidad.

The Youth Hostel is housed in a building that was once used for splitting the slate which was quarried in extremely dangerous circumstances from Gull Point. Waste slate can be seen below the hostel. It is an excellent place to stay. Further along the coast, Lye Rock was once the home of Cornwall's largest colony of puffins. The steep cliffs make good nesting sites for fulmars, guillemots, razorbills and shags. Caves could be used for breeding by seals. Their numbers were drastically reduced in the 19th century, when fishermen demanded their culling and their oil and skins were valuable.

Turning inland up Rocky Valley, the mystery of this area deepens. The fast flowing stream, has eroded the steep sided valley formed of soft slate. There was a mill here until about 1900 and the former name of the valley was Millcoombe. Behind a ruined building are two labyrinths carved into the rock face. They are each about nine inches in diameter. They are claimed to be two labyrinths of original Cretean design, dating from about 1500 BC (when Cretean civilisation collapsed and survivors may have brought their labyrinth cult here).

The distinctive herringbone style of the slate walls of this region has also been linked to Crete. It is hard to be sure, however. They may have been carved by a miller. Perhaps they are related to the labyrinth carved on a slate and on view in the Witchcraft Museum in Boscastle (see Walk 2). This ritual object was donated in 1950 by the daughter of a famous 'wise woman', Kate 'The Gull' Turner, who was given it by a witch from the Isle of Man. Called a Troy Stone, it was used to gain states of altered consciousness. The witch traced her finger over the course of the labyrinth whilst humming, until a transcendent state was reached.

Further up the valley, in St Nectan's wooded glen, it is intriguing to compare the saint's name with that of the old Celtic Water God, Nudd, Nodens or Nechtan. It is the perfect setting for nymphs.

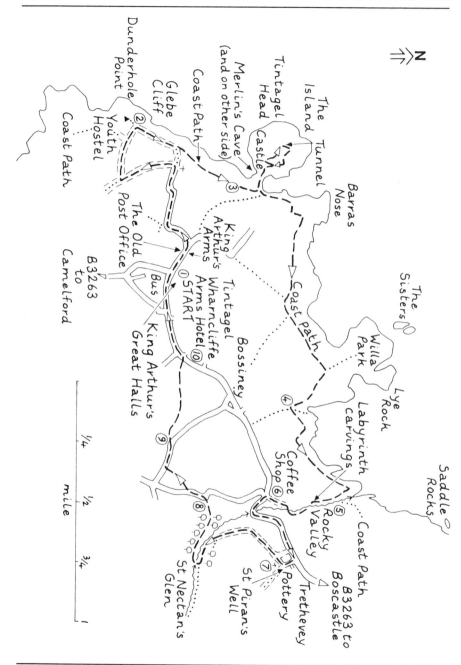

The Walk

1. Go right to reach the King Arthur's Arms on your right. Across the road, on your left, is the Old Post Office. Go ahead to a road junction. Turn left down the road signposted for St Materiana's Church and Glebe Cliff (and a sign at ground level points towards the Youth Hostel). Visit the church (the Roman milestone is on the west wall of the south transept). Continue to the area for car parking and turn left along a rough lane. Turn right at a lane junction, towards the sea. Bear right at a fork.

2. Turn right along the rough lane, away from the Youth Hostel (down on your left). When the track bends right to the church, go straight ahead along the cliff top path.

3. Cross a slate stile and follow a wall on your left down to an entrance to Tintagel Castle, on your left. This is in the care of English Heritage, is open daily (except Mondays in winter and over Christmas and on New Year's Day) between 10 am and 6 pm (4pm in the winter). There is an admission charge (or you could use your season ticket, which can be purchased at this site).

Explore The Island, as it is called, taking the path which climbs to the Chapel ruins, then to the Garden and a mysterious tunnel. Return to the medieval castle's Inner Ward. Descend to the wooden bridge and return across it to the 'mainland'. Fork left along the lower path and reach an English Heritage Shop and Exhibition Centre, opposite a cafe (selling Cornish pasties that would cover the biggest of dinner plates). Continue along the Coast Path, above the sea on your left.

4. Cross a footbridge over a stream and follow the Coast Path up steps. Continue over a stile, ignore a path going inland on your right (and down to the cove on your left) and go ahead with the Coast Path up more steps.

5. Do not follow the Coast Path across a footbridge. Turn right up Rocky Valley along the signposted path to Trevillet Mill and Coffee Shop. Walk upstream and turn left over another footbridge. Follow the path to the mill ruins. Divert left behind the ruin of one old mill building to see two rock carved labyrinths. Resume the path that goes upstream, above the stream on your right. Turn right over the next footbridge to the Coffee Shop. Continue up its access lane to the B3263 road.

6. Go left along the road. Reach a letter box on your right (where there should be a telephone box on your left according to a 'T' on the O.S. Pathfinder Map but isn't because it has been – perhaps temporarily – removed). Take the track on your right to pass St Nectan's Pottery on your left. Reach St Piran's Church. Notice the old holy well, now surmounted by an iron cross, opposite the church.

7. Fork right along a metalled lane which is signposted as a Public Footpath. Pass St Piran's Nursery on your right. Go down its path to see an old Roman milestone (from the time of the joint Emperors Gallus and Volucianus, 251-253 AD) at the bottom on your right. Continue along the lane past houses, then as a footpath through trees. Reach a footbridge and turn right across it. Bear right along a path which emerges from the woodland of St Nectan's Glen at a kissing gate. Go ahead along a well-trodden fieldpath to a road.

8. Turn left along the road for 200 yards, then turn right over a slate stile to follow a signposted fieldpath. Head towards farm buildings, being joined halfway by a hedge on your right. Cross a waymarked stile in a wall to pass a house on your left and reach a road. Turn right along it.

9. As the road bends slightly right, fork left to a field gate. Go through it and walk beside the hedge on your left for 50 yards. Bear right to a stile in the hedge opposite, some 50 yards from the corner. Continue across a field to the next stile. Go over one more field to reach a road.

10. Turn left through Tintagel. Reach King Arthur's Great Halls, then the Wharncliff Arms Hotel, on your right.

4. Padstow

Route: Padstow – Saints Way – Little Petherick – St. Issey – Camel Trail – Padstow.

Distance: $7^1/_2$ miles.

Map: O.S. Pathfinder 1337 Padstow and Wadebridge.

Start: The Golden Lion, Padstow (Grid Reference SW918754).

Access: Anybody stuck in a traffic jam coming here will mourn the loss of the railway. The station survives near Padstow's harbour and it is best to park nearby. The No. 55 bus provides a link with British Rail at Bodmin Parkway on weekdays. Curiously, there is no Saturday bus service between Padstow and Newquay, but the No. 56 bus runs between the two places from Mondays to Fridays and the No. 56A bus runs between Newquay and Wadebridge via Padstow on summer Sundays and Bank Holiday Mondays.

The Golden Lion (01841 532797)

This is where the original (red ribbon) Old 'Obby 'Oss is stabled, and where the BBC filmed their documentary in 1953. An old pub which may have been cottages in the 16th century, it is frequented by personalities as diverse as the former England wicket keeper Alan Knott and ITV's newsreader Peter Snow. Cornish Original is just one of the Real Ales on offer, while food is available. Opening hours are 11 am to 3 pm and 6 pm to 11 pm on weekdays, noon to 3 pm and 7 pm to 10.30 pm on Sundays.

Padstow

This was already a flourishing fishing village when St. Petroc came from Ireland (or Dyfed?) in the sixth century and founded a Celtic llan or sacred enclosure here (to use the word monastery might only serve to confuse with stone buildings). The gradual silting up of the Camel

Padstow Harbour

Estuary halted the development of the port. The first train arrived on 27th March, 1899. Padstow became the western outpost of the London and South-Western Railway, being 259 $^1/_2$ miles from Waterloo Station. Perhaps the fact that it wasn't an old Great Western Railway line led to its closure on 30th January, 1967. The line was viable, but it seems that British Rail's Western Region had to find a sacrificial lamb to appease those who were too short-sighted to see the value of railways.

Padstow remains unspoilt by tourism. There are lots of visitors, but they tend to pass through. The lack of a beach must help to deter them. It is as if the place is meant to preserve its ancient identity, which is an extremely deep one in a superficial world. It is manifested every 1st May (the old Beltane) by Padstow's famous Hobby Horse, or 'Obby 'Oss. This does not take to the streets to attract tourists. Its dance is a fiercely-maintained local tradition dating back so far that it has been called the oldest in Britain. Come and watch, but you'll never truly partake in this event as a visitor. You may feel like an intruder. A little of the spirt was captured on film by the BBC in 1953. The grainy black and white film includes the night concert in the Golden Lion pub. I was lucky enough to see this film and hear its producer talk about making it when he showed it to the Ley Hunters' Moot in 1989.

If you are lucky enough to see it, notice the drummer in the pub during the evening concert. The shamanic beat of his drum is accompanied by the eyes of a man possessed by the very spirit of the living earth. Similarly, so are the eyes of the dancers. Such intensity is alien to the blandness of modern life, where the ancient holy days have become mere holidays. In my experience, only the passion of an Orange band on the 12th July in Belfast could be compared to it.

There are in fact three 'Osses. The original Old 'Oss has a red ribbon and is stabled at the Golden Lion Inn. The second is a Temperance 'Oss, marked by a blue ribbon. Nowadays, I am assured, its 'temperance' is decidedly theoretical. Thirdly, there is a small Children's 'Oss. May Day here is our living heritage. It has survived because the locals have been strongly loyal to their traditions. Long may it continue!

Interestingly, St. Petroc removed a splinter from the eye of a local 'dragon'. As elsewhere, could the horse and dragon be the same? The South Door of St. Petroc's Church, Padstow, is the start of the Saints Way ('Forth an Syns' in Cornish). This long distance path runs for some 26 miles to Fowey and was used in ancient times as an alternative to the sea passage around Land's End.

The Walk

1. Go left along Church Lane to Padstow's St. Petroc's Church. Leave by the lychgate opposite the south porch. Follow the waymarked Saints Way along a shaded metalled path that reveals the name Hill Street at its end. Go ahead across New Street and fork right up Dennis Road. Continue down Dennis Lane (a No Through Road). pass paths and a lake on your left.

2. Turn left along the Saints Way. This signposted path soon turns right. Go through a fieldgate and follow the signposted path uphill with a hedge on your right. Notice the obelisk on Dennis Hill. Dennis is derived from dinas, meaning fort (there is a hillfort). The obelisk was erected in 1887 and is 50 feet high, with each foot marking one year of Queen Victoria's reign. Turn right over the waymarked stile in the top corner. Turn left immediately to follow the hedge on your left down to a stile.

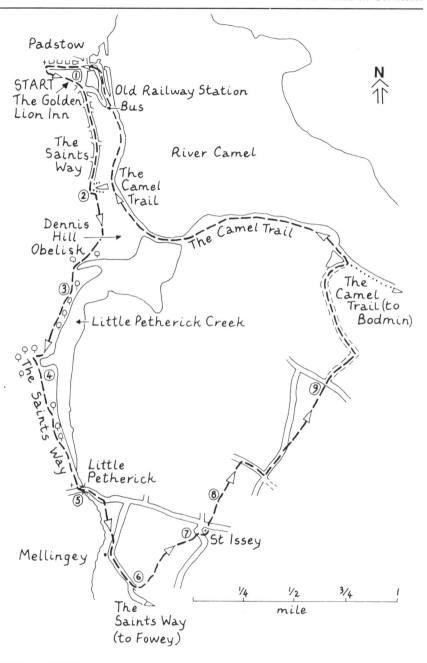

Padstow

START
The Golden
Lion Inn

Old Railway Station
Bus

The
Saints
Way

The
Camel
Trail

River Camel

N

Dennis
Hill
Obelisk

The Camel Trail

The
Camel
Trail (to
Bodmin)

Little Petherick Creek

The Saints Way

Little
Petherick

Mellingey

St Issey

The
Saints Way
(to Fowey)

¼   ½   ¾   1
mile

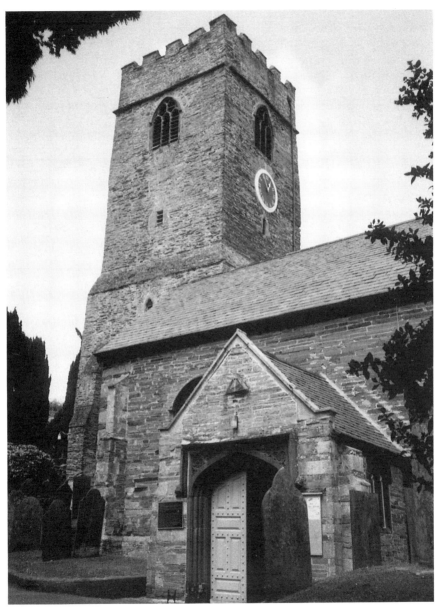

St. Petroc's Church, Padstow

Bear right, as waymarked, downhill to woodland. Take a path down to a footbridge over a stream at the head of a creek. Go right, as waymarked then left up steps to a field. Walk with a hedge on you right. Turn right over a stile in the corner.

3. Turn left to walk above bushes and Little Petherick Creek on your left. Pass three fields on your right, linked by stiles. Take the waymarked path downhill in the third corner. Pass an inlet on your left. Cross a stile, two wooden footbridges and climb steps to go over another stile.

4. Turn right, as waymarked, to climb to another waymark post. Bear right along a shady track. Cut across the corner of the field on your left to a waymark post. Go right, beside the hedge on your right, and cross a stile into woodland. Follow the woodland path which eventually bears left down steps to a stile. Continue to reach the road at Little Petherick. The church is on your right.

5. Turn left to follow the road over the bridge and uphill. Turn right over a stone stile to follow the signposted public footpath down to a Saints Way waymark post. Go left into the next field. Walk along its foot, following a hedge on your right. Cross the next field to reach a road. Go right into Mellingey. Pass the mill (melin in Cornish) which gives this place its name, on your right. It is now a craft centre and offers refreshments. Pass a trout farm on your left.

6. Leave the Saints Way by forking left along a signposted public footpath. Reach a waymark post which has a small green circle as well as a yellow arrow. Take the stone steps to cross a high stile and enter a field. Bear left to follow a waymarked path over stepping stones and a footbridge in the shade of trees. Continue uphill, keeping the hedge on your left. Aim for St. Issey's church tower. Go left, as waymarked, in the farmyard before it.

7. Go right along the road. Turn left to St. Issey's Church (perhaps dedicated to one of King Brychan's 24 daughters, or one of his 12 sons – Brychan was of Irish descent but ruled in the modern Brecon district of South Wales). Leave by the north gate, cross the road to the bus shelter and turn left for 50 yards to a signpost. Turn right through a gate to follow the public footpath. Cut across a corner of a field to take a stile in the hedge on your right. Bear left to a stile and footbridge at the bottom of the next field.

8. Bear slightly right over a field to take a waymarked gap ahead. Follow a hedge on your right to a stile giving access to a road. Turn right to a T junction. Turn left downhill. Fork right through the second fieldgate on your right, marked by a public footpath signpost. Descend to cross a stream by a grass-covered bridge and go over a stile into the next field. Climb with a hedge on your left to a gate giving access to another road.

9. Cross the road to go ahead down the No Through Road signposted for Old Town Cove. Go up steps at its end to turn left along the line of the dismantled railway which now forms the Camel Trail. This leads to the old railway station in Padstow, by the bus station. Continue past the harbour on your right. Bear left in The Square and go up Lanadwell Street to the Golden Lion Inn on your left.

5. *Jamaica Inn and Brown Willy*

Route: Jamaica Inn – Leskernick Stone Circle – Brown Willy – Leskernick Stone Circle – Jamaica Inn

Distance: 9 miles

Map: O.S. Pathfinder 1338 Bodmin Moor (West)

Start: Jamaica Inn, Bolventor (Grid Reference SX 183767)

Access: The Jamaica Inn is a popular place for motorists to halt at as they take the A30 between Bodmin and Launceston. There is an infrequent bus service. The No. X3 bus between Truro and Bude (via Bodmin and Launceston) stops here on Tuesdays and Saturdays in the summer. Telephone 0872 40404 for times.

Jamaica Inn 01566 86250

Daphne du Maurier's novel has made this one of the most famous pubs in the world. Unfortunately, it hasn't been able to resist the temptation to cash in as a tourist attraction. Nevertheless, the staff are very friendly and Mr Potter's Museum of Curiosity next door can be ignored. The Dame Daphne du Maurier room is worth a visit, if only to see the novelist's typewriter.

The inn was built in 1547 and was a farm, then a Temperance House (serving soft drinks, teas and coffees) before becoming an inn. It was supposedly named by a retired Governor of Jamaica. There is a resident parrot named Percy (an

elderly female). The ghost of a man who was murdered in the 18th century is seen at intervals.

Bed and breakdast accommodation is available, while real ale and food are served. Bar opening hours are 11 am to 11 pm on weekdays, noon to 3 pm and 7 pm to 10.30 pm on Sundays.

The Novel

Daphne du Maurier was inspired to write the famous novel 'Jamaica Inn' after staying here in 1930. It expresses the spirit of the place and years later she was able to write that

'Nothing has really changed since Mary Yellan walked the moors, climbed the tors, and rested in the low dips beside the springs and streams'.

First published in 1936, the novel was soon made into a film by Alfred Hitchcock. Set in the 1700s, the heroine is Mary Yelland. Recently orphaned, she has to leave her house at Helford to live with her aunt on the moorland road between Bodmin and Launceston. Aunt Patience suffers under her husband Joss Merlyn, a smuggler and a murderer. Descriptions of the moor conjure up the image of a hostile environment, unfamiliar to the young girl cast adrift here. Sent to bed by Uncle Joss, Mary witnesses the smugglers at work through a crack in the blind. Unfortunately J.B. Priestley was instructed to write the film script making the squire the head of the smugglers, whereas it is the parson in the book. This enabled Charles Laughton to be the star. The film helped popularise du Maurier's books throughout the world.

The Walk

N.B. BRING A MAP AND COMPASS AND KNOW HOW TO USE THEM!

1. Go left, ignore a No Through Road that comes first on your left but turn left at the next road, which goes under the A30. Bear left with it to a junction and turn right along a lane going away from the A30. Pass another No Through Road, then the access track to Dairywell on your left.

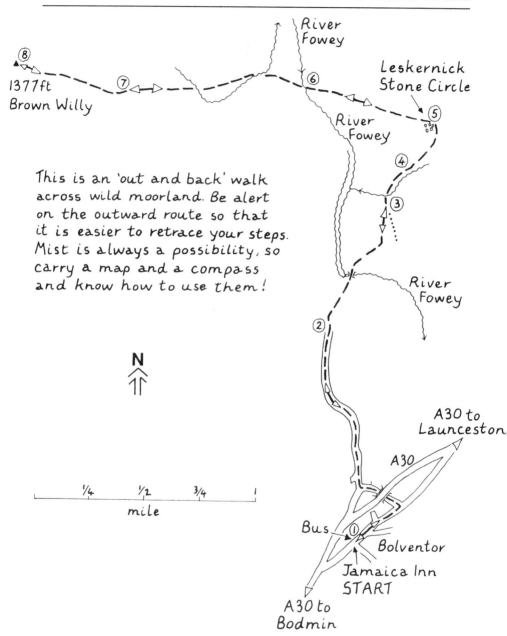

River
Fowey

Leskernick
Stone Circle

⑧
1377ft
Brown Willy

⑦

⑥

⑤

River
Fowey

④

This is an 'out and back' walk
across wild moorland. Be alert
on the outward route so that
it is easier to retrace your steps.
Mist is always a possibility, so
carry a map and a compass
and know how to use them!

③

River
Fowey

②

N

A30 to
Launceston

A30

¼   ½   ¾   I

mile

Bus

①

Bolventor

Jamaica Inn
START

A30 to
Bodmin

2. Go ahead through the gate at the end of the lane. Follow a rough track past the access track to Blackhill on your right, then fork right, away from the access track to Codda on your left. Cross a metal footbridge to the right of a ford and take the gate ahead. Follow the track, waymarked as a bridleway with a blue arrow and, for some special reason, an orange circle. Bear left, as waymarked. Come to a small wooden gate, near another waymark post.

3. Turn left before the small wooden gate (which you do not go through). Walk with a fence on your right to a gate in the corner. Go ahead through it and over a steam. Bear right with the track, walking with the stream on your right.

4. When the stream bears right, bear very slightly left and look for a recumbent stone circle. This is Leskernick Stone Circle, at grid reference SX18817961. It is clearly visible on the flat moorland and appears to have 19 stones (all fallen) plus another stone just outside the circle, to the south-east. John Barnatt, the archaeologist (cf Lesser known Stone Circles in Cornwall, Cornish Archaeology No. 19, 1980), thinks there may be the stump of another stone. The original figure was probably 31 stones and this almost true circle has a diameter of roughly 100 feet.

5. Now you will need your map and compass! It's quite simple really. Aim west (270 degrees) and see the jagged outline of Brown Willy two miles away. At 1377 feet (420 metres), this is the highest point in Cornwall. Head for it, after half a mile with the company of a wall which comes from your left and changes into a fence.

6. Ford a stream (the infant River Fowey) ahead and continue along a rough track going parallel to the fence on your left. Meet a stream (the Fowey) flowing on your right and walk upstream. Bear slightly right across it to pass a wall (or dam?) on your left. Go ahead towards Brown Willy. Cross the stream (Fowey) again, it having made a large bend. Aim just to the left of Brown Willy Tor.

7. Go through a gap in the wall ahead. This is immediately followed by the official access point to this Site of Special Scientific Interest. The path across this private land is a permissive one and you may have to avoid adders. Go ahead over the stile to the right of the small wooden gate. Bear right along a well-trodden path to the summit of Brown Willy.

8. Retrace your steps to the Jamaica Inn. Remember to reverse your compass bearings, initially going east, then turning south to the lane.

The view of Rough Tor from the summit of Brown Willy

6. Bodmin

Route: Bodmin- Camel Trail – Nanstallon – Gilbert's Monument – Bodmin.

Distance: $6^1/_2$ miles.

Map: O.S. Pathfinder 1347 Bodmin.

Start: The Hole in the Wall, Bodmin (Grid Reference SX072671).

Access: There is a car park behind this pub in the centre of Bodmin. The bus stop at Mount Folly is served by a host of buses, including No. 55 between Bodmin Parkway and Padstow, No. X3 between Truro and Bude via Tintagel and No. X4 between Truro and Bude via Launceston. Try to arrive in Bodmin by steam train on the Bodmin and Wenford Railway. This connects with British Rail at Bodmin Parkway and brings 'customers' (as rail passengers must now be called) to Bodmin General. The service is seasonal, so telephone 01208 73666 for details.

The Hole in the Wall (01208 72397)

There used to be a hole in the wall here through which food, drink and supplies were passed to debtors in the old debtors' prison. This was established by the 18th century, while the premises had been converted into a pub by the late 19th century. The gaoler used to brew beer to sell to the inmates, who are known to have numbered up to 19 at times. Men, women and children were all kept in just the one cell. John Eyre, pioneer of Congregationalism, was born here. A stuffed lion guards a beer garden which has the town leat flowing through it. Real ale and bar snacks are available, while there is a restaurant. Opening hours are 11 am to 2.30 pm and 5 pm to 11 pm from Mondays to Fridays, 11 am to 11 pm on Saturdays plus noon to 3 pm and 7 pm to 10.30 pm on Sundays.

The Hole in the Wall, Bodmin

Bodmin

Bodmin is derived from Bod-minhi, meaning 'House of Sanctuary'. An early monastery flourished here, well away from Danish coastal raiders. A Welsh missionary called Guron (or Goromus) had started it all in the fifth century, but it is the sixth century Irish missionary, St. Petroc, to whom Bodmin's church (the largest parish church in Cornwall) is dedicated. By 1086, the Domesday Survey found Bodmin to be the only market town in Cornwall. It became the county's first Coinage Town in 1198. Tin was brought here to be stamped, assayed and taxed before sale.

It was also a centre for Cornish resistance to London rule. In 1497, Thomas Flamank led a march on London to protest against taxation to pay for Henry Tudor's war against the Scots. He was hanged at Tyburn. The next year saw Bodmin men supporting the Pretender, Perkin Warbeck, defeated at Exeter. The locals also protested against the introduction of Cranmers's English prayer book in 1549. When the King's Provost came to restore order, he was entertained by the mayor in the Guildhall. After dinner, the mayor was asked to erect gallows so that one of the rebels could be hanged. When they were set up, the Provost asked the mayor if he thought they were strong enough. When the mayor agreed, the Provost replied, *'Then get you up, for they are for you!'*

Civic pride met a happier fate in 1716, when the County Assizes were held here, instead of in Launceston. The County Gaol (complete with treadmill) was built in 1779, bringing the spectacle of public executions (in the 19th century thousands were to come by special trains to witness these). Finally, in 1836, an Act of Parliament established Bodmin as the county town of Cornwall, instead of Launceston. It has retained this title, despite Truro being chosen for the county's cathedral in 1887. County Hall was also built in Truro in 1889 and the final nail in Bodmin's coffin came with the recent opening of the new Assize Courts in Truro.

Truro was on the Great Western Railway's mainline between London Paddington and Penzance. Bodmin had to make do with a station called Bodmin Road (now Bodmin Parkway) at a distance of three and a half miles from its centre. Yet, Cornish steam railways began here! A standard gauge (4 ft. 8 $\frac{1}{2}$ ins.) railway linked Bodmin with the port of Wadebridge in 1834. This ran from Bodmin North station (its site is now occupied by a supermarket) along what has become the Camel Trail (named after the Cornish river, not the desert animal) to Dunmere. Here it joined the line from Wenfordbridge, whose mineral traffic caused this railway to be built. China clay was carried by British Rail from Wenfordbridge until 1983.

A copper and iron mine was situated at the next junction, in Boscarne. This is where the Great Western Railway from Bodmin Road via Bodmin General finally met the earlier railway. This link, though started in 1847, wasn't opened until 1887. Steam trains are now reviving it. The railway finally reached Padstow in 1899, but passenger services were withdrawn in 1967 and the Camel Trail now provides an easy through walking and cycling route. The local tin trade attracted the Romans, who built a fort at Nanstallon in the first century. This hamlet's name refers to the Valley of the Alan (as the Lower Camel used to be called). The military theme recurs on Beacon Hill, overlooking Bodmin. The 144 ft. high obelisk was erected in 1857 as a memorial to Walter Raleigh Gilbert, a local soldier of famous descent (hence the Christian names) who conquered the Sikhs in India. The town also houses the regimental museum of the Devon and Cornwall Light Infantry.

The Walk

1. Go left and left again along Dennison Road. Fork right (as signposted for Bodmin Gaol) up Berrycombe Road. Pass the fire station on your left. Pass the Gaol on your right. Walk with a playing field on your left.

2. Reach the car park at the start of the Camel Trail. Walk along the line of the dismantled railway from Bodmin North. This starts by going under a road bridge. Continue past the old Dunmere Halt after a second road bridge.

3. Reach a signposted junction. Go ahead towards Wadebridge (ignoring the route to Poley's Bridge on your right). Cross a bridge over the River Camel. Reach Boscarne Junction, where the rails of the Bodmin and Wenford Railway end on your left. Go ahead to the old halt at Nanstallon.

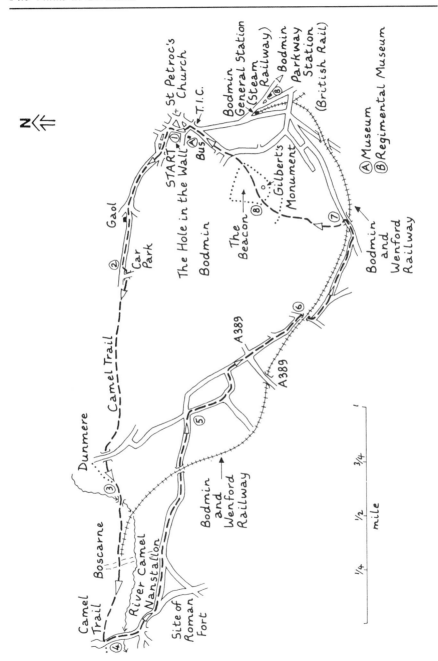

4. Leave the Camel Trail by turning left down the road to Nanstallon. Cross the River Camel. Bear left at a road junction and fork left in the village. Keep left at the next road junction. Go under a railway bridge

5. Turn right at a crossroads. Go left at the next junction and turn right at a T junction. Reach the A389 and cross it carefully to continue up Westheath Road, ahead. Pass Queen's Crescent on your left.

6. Turn right under the railway bridge, then turn left along Kirland Road. Fork left up Gladstone Road. Bear left with Crabtree Lane to cross the bridge over the railway.

7. Turn left along a signposted public footpath. Reach the corner of the field and turn right to walk beside the hedge on your right. Take the gap in the corner ahead and pass a second field on your left. Continue over a stone stile, follow the hedge on your right and cross another stile. Go ahead across one track, to maintain your direction up another.

8. Fork right along the middle of three tracks ahead. Pass Gilbert's Monument on your right. Aim for the far right corner of this open plateau. Take the descending path ahead. Emerge at Beacon Road. Cross it carefully to go ahead down Crinnicks Hill. Pass the bus shelter at Mount Folly on your left and the Tourist Information Centre on your right. Go left into Mount Folly Square and turn right down Crockwell Street (past the Midland Bank at its corner on your left). The Hole in the Wall is on your left.

7. Lostwithiel

Route: Lostwithiel – Restormel Castle – Lanhydrock House – Saints Way – Helman Tor – Lanlivery – Lostwithiel

Distance: 12 miles

Maps: O.S. Pathfinders 1347 Bodmin and 1354 St Austell and Fowey

Start: The Globe Inn, Lostwithiel (Grid Reference SX 105598)

Access: Lostwithiel has a station on British Rail's mainline between Plymouth and Penzance.

The Globe Inn (01208 872501)

The River Fowey ran under this pub when it was built in the 13th century. It was once the home of the Norway family, to which the novelist Neville Shute belongs. The present name was acquired when a British packet captained by a member of the Norway family fought a gallant action against the larger American privateer 'The Globe'. This was on 13th November, 1813 and Captain Norway's 32 men took on over 100 Americans, who also had more and heavier guns. 'The Montagu' was boarded by 39 Americans, of whom 37 were killed by the British and two captured. A further 19 Americans were wounded. The captain of 'The Montagu', John Norway, was one of the British dead. His spirit lives on in the form of whole-hearted hospitality at this pub. Real ale is served, while accommodation is available. There is a restaurant and a beer garden. Opening hours are 11.30 am to 3 pm and 6 pm to 11 pm on weekdays, noon to 3 pm and 7 pm to 10.30 pm on Sundays.

Lostwithiel

This was, briefly, the capital of Cornwall in the 13th century (before the honour went to Launceston). The bureaucrats were housed in the Great Hall. Tin was weighed here and a corner (coin) of each ingot was melted and assayed (tested for quality).

The Globe Inn, Lostwithiel

Courts were held in the Convocation Hall, which was sold to the Freemasons in 1878. This was never the 'Old Duchy Palace', however. The Duchy of Cornwall wasn't created until 1337, when Edward III's eldest son, the Black Prince, rode to Launceston Castle to be proclaimed

The 'Green Man' gargoyle

the first Duke of Cornwall. He only visited Lostwithiel once or twice and stayed at Restormel Castle. This is a significant spot, however, especially if your feet take you to St Bartholomew's Church. Built in 1190 on an ancient religious site, this is on the energy lines described by Hamish Miller and Paul Broadhurst in their Book 'The Sun and the Serpent' (1989). Of particular interest is the 14th century font. One of the carvings is a remarkable gargoyle. The roof of the church was blown up by Parliamentarians in the Civil War. They also stabled their horses here and christened one 'Charles' in the font. The tower used to have open archways because it was built over an ancient right of way.

Restormel Castle

The Normans built on this strategic spot and Edgar, Earl of Cornwall, rebuilt the castle in the middle ages. Garrisoned by both sides in the Civil War, Restormel is now in the care of English Heritage. It is open between April and September daily, from 10 am to 6 pm.

Lanhydrock

The Robartes family made this their home from 1620 until their line ran out in 1969, by which time the house and grounds had been in the care of the National Trust for 16 years. Supporters of the Parliamentary cause, they allowed the Earl of Essex to make it his headquarters during the

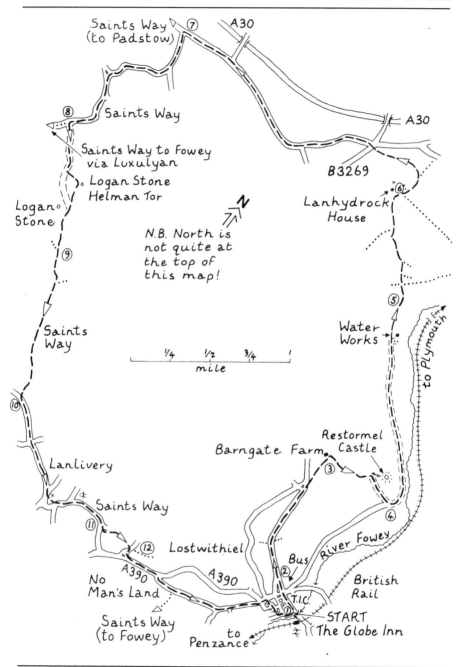

Saints Way
(to Padstow) (7)   A30

(8)   Saints Way

Saints Way to Fowey
via Luxulyan

Logan Stone
Helman Tor

Logan
Stone

(9)

A30

B3269

Lanhydrock
House

(6)

N

N.B. North is
not quite at
the top of
this map!

Saints
Way

Water
Works

(5)

to Plymouth

¼   ½   ¾   1

mile

(10)

Restormel
Castle

Barngate Farm

(3)

Lanlivery

Saints Way

River Fowey

(4)

(11)

(12)   Lostwithiel

A390

A390

No
Man's Land

Saints Way
(to Fowey)

to
Penzance

Bus

(2)

British
Rail

T.I.C.

(1)

START
The Globe Inn

Civil War. Royalists captured it in 1644. Real disaster had to wait until 1881, however, when the 17th century house was largely destroyed by a fire. It was faithfully rebuilt by the current Lord Robartes as *'a simple family home'*. There is a delightful 22 acre garden, with magnificent camellias, magnolias and rhododendrons. Nearby is the 15th century church of St Hydroc (the original manor house belonged to the Austinians from the Priory of St Petroc at Bodmin).

The property's greatest treasure is 1000 acres of grazed grassland and deciduous woodland, through which run a network of footpaths. Thomas Hardy must have wandered this way with his Emma. Lanhydrock House has been identified as the principal original of 'Endelstow House' in his novel 'A Pair of Blue Eyes'. Here are the *'spacious court'*, the *'ancient gate-house of dun stone'*, the many-mullioned windows, the avenue of trees and the long barrel-vaulted picture gallery.

The house is open between April and November from Tuesdays to Sundays (plus Bank Holiday Mondays) between 11 am and 5.30 pm (4.30 pm in October).

Lanlivery

The church is another place visited by the energy line followed by Miller and Broadhurst (op cit). It stands on a mound and has a 97 feet high tower. This forms a notable landmark across the wild moorland. Its presence didn't stop the notorious Tregeagle getting drunk and selling his soul to the devil here, however, so don't go one over the eight! Helman Tor, with its rocking logan stone, provides dramatic views over mid-Cornwall.

The Walk

1. Go left up North Street. Visit St Bartholomew's Church on your left. Return to North Street and continue up it to the A390. Bus stops and the Tourist Information Centre (in a Community Centre) stand on your right. Go ahead across the main road and up Duke Street.

2. Go right, uphill. As the road bears left to approach a junction with the

B3268 at Hillhead, fork right through a wooden gate and along a grassy track (signposted as a Public Footpath). Continue over a ladder stile beside a gate and go ahead beside a hedge on your left.

3. When you are level with Barngate Farm, on your left, turn right over a stile. Turn left in the field to reach a ladder stile on its corner. Cross this and turn right to walk beside a hedge on your right. Continue over a ladder stile to the right of a gate in the bottom hedge. Descend with the hedge on your right to the car park of Restormel Castle. Visit the castle, on your left, then go down its access road.

Restormel Castle

4. Turn left at the lane junction. Pass a waterworks on your right. Continue along a rough track, taking the gate into a field and following the fence on your left to a gate in the opposite hedge. Go ahead through it and along the track to a gate in the perimeter wall of woodland.

5. Enter the woodland and bear left along a shady track. Turn right at its junction with a broad track, but for just 10 yards. Turn left over a stone stile to continue along the woodland path. Follow this path to Lanhydrock House.

The Gatehouse, Lanhydrock

6. With your back to Lanhydrock House, go left from the entrance, along the drive. Fork left at a 'No Exit' sign, to follow the public footpath (Cars go ahead). Reach the B3268 at a roundabout, cross it carefully and go ahead up a lane, passing a telephone box on your right. Continue past a lane on your left, then a lane on your right.

7. Reach an old stone cross and a wooden Saints Way waymark post on your right. Turn left along the lane signposted to Fenton Pits and Trebell Green. Reach another cross and fork right, as waymarked, towards Trebell Green. Fork left at a grassy triangle.

8. Turn left with the eastern branch of the Saints Way along the lane towards Helman Tor. Take a stile on your left to follow the path straight up to the summit. Turn right along the ridge and down to a car park. Go left along the lane, which soon deteriorates to a rough track.

9. Ignore a signposted Public Footpath going right. Take the waymarked Saints Way ahead. Emerge through a gate which is waymarked by a blue arrow. Continue along a fenced track. Reach the re-erected Menawink Cross, discovered in 1990, just before a gate giving access to a road.

10. Go left along the road to Lanlivery. Take the path through the churchyard to pass the porch of St Brevita's Church on your left. Leave by the east gate and turn left along a road (away from the junction on your right). Fork right on the descending road. Pass Powderham Castle Tourist Park (for caravans) on your left.

11. When the road bends right, pass Pelyntor Cottage on your left, then turn left up steps to a small gate. Go ahead along the diverted public footpath, which is signposted as going up to the top left corner of this field. Continue through a small wooden gate and over a stone stile. Walk along the waymarked Saints Way with the hedge on your left in the next field.

12. Turn right along a road, still following the waymarked Saints Way. Turn left at a road junction. Walk along the A390 for 300 yards, then fork right to follow a quiet lane down to Lostwithiel. Turn right down South Street, emerge through the archway of the Great Hall and turn left to pass the Convocation Hall on your left. Bear right towards the old bridge over the River Fowey. Go left back to the pub (or right if you want the British Rail Station).

8. The Hurlers and the Cheesewring

Route: Upton Cross – Minions – The Hurlers – Cheesewring – Minions – Upton Cross.

Distance: 5 miles.

Map: O.S. Pathfinder 1339 Bodmin Moor (East) and Kelly Bray.

Start: The Caradon Inn, Upton Cross (Grid Reference SX280723).

Access: There is a reasonably good weekday bus service (No. 278) from Liskeard Railway Station to Upton Cross. There is also a bus (No. 271) on Friday mornings only from Liskeard (Bay Tree Hill – not the railway station) to both Minions and Upton Cross. The return bus is on Friday afternoons only. Cars can be parked at Upton Cross or at a car park on the western edge of Minions, at the start of the track to the Hurlers.

The Caradon Inn (01579 62391)

This is the friendliest of inns, where ramblers are always welcome, however muddy their boots! Perhaps this is a legacy of the old tin-mining days, when the miners were paid (in tokens, exchangeable only at the owner's establishments) here. 17th century cottages were converted into a pub by the early 19th century. There was a Fox and Hounds Inn here in the 1830s.

By the late 19th century, this had become the Caradon Hotel. The Vennings Brewery of Liskeard owned it until they were bought by a major brewer around 1960. This inn was then sold and is now a free-house. It stands across the road from Sterts moorland open-air theatre and gallery. This offers an excellent programme and an evening here would make a memorable end to a day's rambling. Covered seats can be booked in advance (Tel. 01579 62382/62962), while the ice-cream stall also hires out blankets!

Real ale and bar snacks are available. The bar opening hours are 11.45 am to 3 pm and 5.30 pm to 11 pm on weekdays, noon to 3 pm and 7 pm to 10.30 pm on Sundays. There is an authentic ghost story, told by a very

The Caradon Inn, Upton Cross

old regular. He used to live here and gave his parents the slip on Saturday nights by escaping through his bedroom window at a signal from his friend outside. One day his friend left for London on his motorcycle. That night, however, the window was knocked in the usual way. Nobody was there and the noise remained a mystery until news reached Cornwall of his friend's death – at the time of the knocking on the window.

The Cheesewring Hotel (01579 62321)

At a height of 995 feet above sea level, this claims to be the highest pub in Cornwall. It is famous for its food, accommodation and real ale. Peacocks roam the garden, while ghostly steps are often heard at night. The hotel dates from the 19th century and the bar's opening hours are 11 am to 11 pm on weekdays, noon to 3 pm and 7 pm to 10.30 pm on Sundays.

The Minions Moor

Weeks of glorious sunshine were replaced by heavy rain when I came here. That's why this walk is the simplest of affairs. It fulfils the essential visits to the Hurlers and the Cheesewring. This part of Bodmin Moor has much more to offer, however. It will be explored on future visits to Cornwall. Sheltering in the Post Office at Minions, I bought an excellent local guide book by Peter Stanier. Entitled 'The Minions Moor', it should be available locally for about £3 and describes several local walks – perfect for a sunny day!

The Hurlers

Legend states that the game of hurling (once as common in Cornwall as it is in Ireland today) was played here. Unfortunately, the games took place on a Sunday, which led to the Sabbath-breakers being turned to stone. There must have been three games going on simultaneously, as there are three stone circles. Two isolated stones are the unfortunate Pipers or Watchers, whose only crime was to support their team on a Sunday. The first, southernmost, circle is easily missed as it only has two stones left upright. The circles vary in diameter from 108 feet to 140 feet and are a mystery. They do line up with Rillaton Barrow and Stowes Hill. The dowser Hamish Miller discovered that Michael (male) and Mary (female) energy lines cross in the second circle and writes about this (with Paul Broadhurst) in 'The Sun and the Serpent' (1989).

Rillaton Barrow

There is an old legend associated with this too. A druid used to offer passers-by a drink from a golden cup that could never be emptied. One day a hunter was determined to drain the cup. His horse threw him and he was buried with the cup. In 1818 the skeleton of a man was found here, together with a golden cup dating from about 1500 BC. The cup is now in the British Museum, with a copy in the County Museum, Truro.

Daniel Gumb's Cave

This is a Victorian reconstruction of the cave-dwelling of a stone-cutter, mystic and philosopher who lived here with his family before the area was mined, quarried and populated. A section of a door-post has 'D Gumb 1735' carved on it, which may be when he married. He died in 1776. Famous for being able to predict the future and for spending his nights 'learning the customs of the stars', he was responsible for the geometrical carving on a roof stone. Hamish Miller (op.cit.) has found that the Michael energy line goes through his cave. Perhaps he was a druid. He certainly chose the simple life. His family home was beneath a 30 foot long granite slab. Quarrying disturbed this, so it is hard to tell exactly what his wife and children had to put up with. They didn't have to worry about a mortgage, poll tax or electricity bill, of course.

The Cheesewring

This is a pillar of granite rings piled 25 feet high. A natural formation, it is a result of the erosion of softer surrounding rocks. John Michell's famous St. Michael or dragon line from Carn lês Boel via Glastonbury Tor, Avebury, Royston and Bury St. Edmunds to the Norfolk Coast at Hopton runs through it. Read about this in John Michell's 'New View Over Atlantis'. The old Quarry immediately below it is now alive with young people (naval recruits, scouts etc.) learning to abseil on its 150 foot high walls. Granite from here was taken by horse-drawn trains in the 1840s down to Liskeard, then by canal to Looe. Over 100 men and boys were employed and Westmins-ter Bridge was built from it. Steam trains eventually took over, but the demise of the quarry led to the closure of the railway between here and Lis-keard in 1916.

The Walk

1. Go right to the crossroads and turn right to pass the school. Follow the road to Minions.

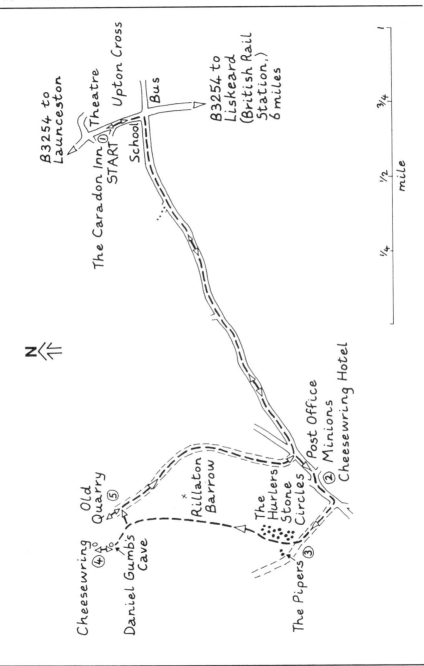

2. Reach the Cheesewring Hotel on your left. Continue through the village and turn right along the track over Bodmin Moor towards the Hurlers.

3. Bear right through the three stone circles of the Hurlers. Pass Rillaton Barrow on your right. Aim for the distinctive Cheesewring perched above the old quarry. Look for Daniel Gumb's Cave about 100 yards south of the Cheesewring on the edge of a flat area to the west of the quarry.

4. Admire the view from the Cheesewring (said to extend 50 miles to Exmoor), then descend and retrace your steps past the quarry on your left. Depart from your outward route by going left to a track which used to be the old railway line.

5. Visit the quarry, then take the track back to Minions. Go left along the road back to Upton Cross.

9. Calstock

Route: Calstock – Danescombe – Cotehele House – Cotehele Quay – Calstock.

Distance: $4^1/_2$ miles plus a possible extension to a mill.

Map: O.S. Pathfinder 1349 Bere Alston and Plymouth.

Start: The Tamar Inn, Calstock (Grid Reference: SX 435686).

Start: Calstock has a station on British Rail's scenic Tamar Valley Line between Plymouth and Gunnislake. Cornish Rail Rovers are valid on this line, which crosses the border between Devon and Cornwall by the spectacular viaduct immediately south of Calstock. Enthusiastic locals are promoting this useful railway. You can add your support by taking the train to the start of this walk.

The Tamar Inn (01822 832487)

Dating from about 1700, this inn is popular with people using various forms of river-craft, including canoes. Real ale and food are available. The opening hours are noon to 3.30 pm and 6 pm to 11pm from Mondays to Thursdays, 11 am to 11 pm on Fridays and Saturdays, noon to 3 pm and 7 pm to 10.30 pm on Sundays.

Calstock

This was an important inland port in the days of tin and copper mining. The nearby Devon Great Consols mine (across the River Tamar) was the richest copper mine in Europe. The old mine passed by this route was called Cotehele Consols and produced copper and arsenic.

The East Cornwall Mineral Railway was constructed to link the local mines to the River Tamar at Calstock Quay. The line from Kelly Bray, near Callington, to Calstock opened in 1872. It had a gauge of 3 ft. 6 ins. and made the final descent to the quays by a rope-worked incline. This incline (now marked only by a bridge over the road) was replaced by a steam hoist to cope with standard gauge wagons when Calstock was connected to the national rail network by the completion of the viaduct in 1907. This is built of concrete block masonry , which resembles stone in appearance. 11,000 blocks were made on site, on the Devon bank. A search for a solid foundation for one of the river piers caused construction to take three and a half years.

Passenger services started in 1908, bringing connections to Plymouth and, from nearby Bere Alston, to Waterloo (on the London and South-Western Railway). The old narrow gauge line was converted to standard gauge, but the section between Callington and Gunnislake was closed in 1966.

Cotehele House

Come here between April and October, except on Fridays, from 11 am to 5.30 pm, (5 pm in October) to visit this ancient house. It dates from 1353, most of it was built in the Tudor period and was an Edgcumbe family home until given to the National Trust in 1947. The family built a new house at Mount Edgcumbe (see walk 13) in 1553 and this became their second home.

Charles I slept here in 1644, but the gardens weren't laid out until the 1860s. Exotic trees and shrubs shelter in a valley. The chapel attached to the house boasts the third oldest clock in Britain, after those at Salisbury and Wells. Unlike them, however, this one is completely original.

Another chapel (in the wood, overlooking the River Tamar) was built about 1490 by Richard Edgcumbe in gratitude for his safe escape to France in 1483, when he was in danger from the Sir Henry Bodrugan who was later to escape from him near Mevagissey (Walk 16). Visitors to the National Trust property can pick up a free map of Cotehele Estate at Reception and extend this walk to the mill, which dates from the Middle Ages and was rebuilt in the 18th and 19th centuries.

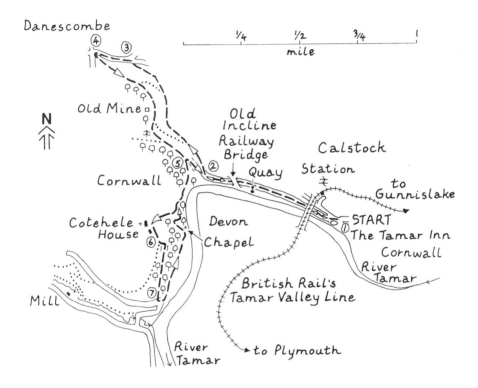

A small Maritime Museum at Cotehele Quay is open at the same time as Cotehele House, plus on Fridays. A restored Tamar sailing barge ('Shamrock') is moored nearby. A former riverside inn houses a cafe and a shop.

The Walk

1. Facing the river, go right, then left up Commercial Road. Soon fork left down a No Through Road to walk above the River Tamar on your left. Go ahead under the railway viaduct and pass Calstock Boat-yard (on your left) and an old limekiln (on your right). Go ahead under the old incline bridge.

2. Pass Danescombe Valley Hotel on your right, then fork right up a track. This passes houses, glasshouses, old smallholdings which produced early crops for the London and South-Western Railway to whisk to London, and becomes a very narrow footpath. Keep climbing, ignoring downhill forks.

3. Reach a road and turn left down it to Danescombe.

4. Just before the hamlet, turn sharply left down a signposted public footpath. Follow a shady path beside a stream on your right. Keep to this path, ignoring side paths. Pass old mine buildings on your right. Cross the stream and continue down a broad track with the stream now on your left.

5. Leave the valley by forking right up the track which is signposted for Cotehele House. Bear right up the higher path at a fork and reach the house on your right.

6. Go through the car park, on your left. Take the access road down to Cotehele Quay.

7. Turn left to pass the museum and walk upstream. Follow the signposted woodland path to Danescombe and Calstock. Pass the chapel in the wood and return to your outward path. Retrace your steps to point 5. Turn sharply right along the track past a marsh on your right. Reach the Danescombe Valley Hotel on your left. Go ahead back to Calstock.

10. *Newquay*

Route: Newquay – Trethellan – The Gannel – Penpol Creek – Coast Path – Holywell – Treago Mill – Crantock – Penpol Creek – The Gannel – Trethellan – Newquay.

Distance: 10 miles.

Maps: O.S. Pathfinder 1436 Newquay and 1352 Perranporth.

Start: The Central Inn, Newquay (Grid Reference: SW 807616).

Access: This delightful walk involves crossing The Gannel. There is a footbridge *at low tide*. At high tide there is a rowing-boat ferry, *from June to September*. Newquay is easy to reach, having the terminus for British Rail's branchline from Par, where connections are made with the London Paddington – Penzance mainline. There are also several bus services, including No. 21 from St. Austell, No. 56 from Padstow, No. 57 from St. Ives, Nos. 90 and 92 from Truro, No. 300 from Truro and, most interestingly, No.87 from Truro and No. 88A from Falmouth. Both Nos. 87 and 88A call at Crantock. If there is a high tide in winter, making it impossible to cross The Gannel by this route, you could bus between Newquay and Crantock and walk a shorter circuit of about 7 miles from Crantock.

The Central Inn (01637 872263)

Real ale and food are available at this pub which was rebuilt in 1859 and caters for the tourist trade. There was a pub here in the 18th century which would have been filled with fishermen and sailors. The opening hours are 11 am to 11 pm on weekdays, noon to 3 pm and 7 pm to 10.30 pm on Sundays.

Newquay

The Victorians turned this into Cornwall's premier resort, especially after the completion of the railway to link it with the mainline at Par in 1874.

The Central Inn, Newquay

Pilchards were landed here, while the port was used by the local china clay industry, as well as silver and lead mines. Rocky headlands and sandy beaches combine to make this coastline enchanting. This walk takes you along some of the best coastal scenery in Britain.

The Kelseys

Prehistoric peoples settled on Kelsy Head, leaving a cliff fort and burial mounds. Keep to the boardwalk over the sand dunes. These are being protected by marram, if feet don't trample it. Legend states that the sand covers a lost city (Langarroc), punished for its dissolute behaviour. It is a fact that bones are often found in this area.

Holywell

A spring in the cave that can be reached at low tide on the north side of Holywell Beach is one holywell, while a second lies across the golf course, near the village.

Crantock

St. Carantoc or Caratocus came from either Wales or Ireland in the fifth century. He founded an oratory, a seat of learning and a place of pilgrimage. This was then a useful port, being on the route between Ireland and Brittany and a landfall here enabled travellers to avoid the hazardous passage around Land's End. By 1352, the religious college was riddled with taverns and brothels. Perhaps this is the substance behind the legend of a punished lost city (Langarroc). Perhaps the legend dates back to prehistory, when the earthworks were dug on Kelsey Head. This is obviously a sacred place, in a magical setting open to divine wrath.

The Walk

1. Go right and right again to pass car parks. Go ahead at a pelican crossing to follow Crantock Street. Turn left at Higher Tower Road. Turn right at a roundabout, up Mount Mise.

2. Turn left down Trethellan Hill (a No Through Road). Go down steps signposted as the public footpath to Cranstock. Turn right at a lower road for 50 yards. Bear left down the signposted public footpath. Go down to The Gannel. *At low tide* there is a footbridge across the river. At

The Gannel, Newquay

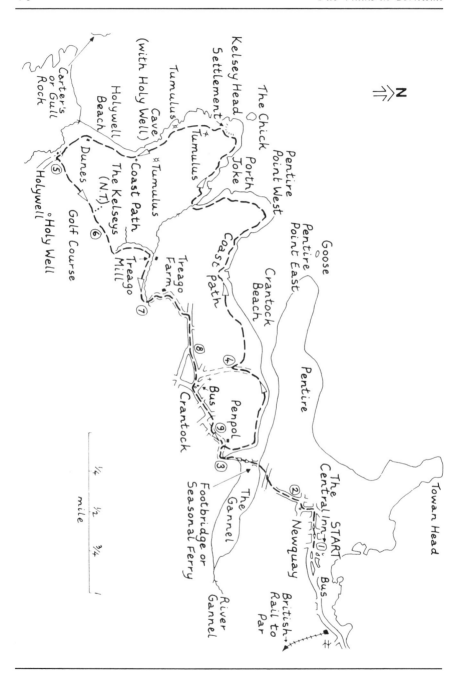

high tide, *in the summer*, there is a rowing-boat ferry. Follow the path up the left side of Penpol Creek, ahead.

3. Turn right over the stepping stones beside the ford at the head of Penpol Creek. Go ahead up the lane. Soon, turn right over a stone stile to the right of a gate with a 'Footpath to Newquay' sign. Go down the field to a kissing gate and go through it to follow a woodland path. Emerge through a second kissing gate to follow the foot of the field on your left, above The Gannel on your right. Bear left down a rough track past bungalows on your right.

4. Turn sharply right with the signposted Coast Path. Go down steps, cross the car park and go up steps to follow the Coast Path along the National Trust land above picturesque Crantock Beach, on your right. Follow the obvious Coast Path around Pentire Point West, Porth Joke (another lovely beach) and Kelsey Head, with its prehistoric earthworks. Follow the board-walk over the dunes down to Holywell Beach. Pass the lifeguard's hut and turn left towards Holywell. Keep the stream on your right, then pass a car park and beach cafe on your right. Go ahead up a metalled path to a shop on your left.

Porth Joke

5. Turn sharply left to follow a path past houses on your right. Follow the fenced path between the dunes and the golf course, which is on your right. Take a small gate ahead. Follow a fence on your right until a fieldgate in it. Turn right through the gate and turn left immediately to walk with the fence now on your left.

6. When the fence turns left, strike out ahead. Reach a gate in a fence coming from your right, above a spring on your left. Turn left to walk above the stream on your left. Bear right to pass Treago Mill on your left.

7. Turn left with the track over a stream. Go up the metalled lane. Pass Treago Farm and reach a road. Turn right to Crantock.

8. Fork left along Gustory Road. Keep right at its junction with a road coming sharply from your left. Pass the bus shelter on your left and take the narrow lane opposite the telephone box. A sign on a telephone pole says 'Footpath to Newquay'. Go ahead over a stile beside a gate in the corner marked by a cross. Bear right across a field to a stile in the far right corner.

9. Go left down a lane. Pass Penpol House, then the stile taken on your outward journey. Retrace your steps back to the pub in Newquay.

11. Fowey

Route: Fowey – St. Catherine's Point – Coast Path – Tregaminion – Tristan Stone – Fowey.

Distance: 8 miles.

Map: O.S. Pathfinder 1354 St. Austell and Fowey.

Start: The Ship Inn, Fowey (Grid Reference SX 125517).

Access: Sir John Betjeman considered Fowey to be *'a haunted town made for sailors and pedestrians'*. It isn't really for motorists. This isn't a problem as there is an excellent bus service (No. 24) from Par, the nearest railway station.

The Ship Inn (0172683 3751)

Betjeman was right. Fowey is haunted. Try bed and breakfast in John Rashleigh's bedroom, known as the Oakroom, in his Ship Inn. Several people have seen the ghost of an old lady there. This room remains as it was originally with ornamental ceiling, fine oak panelled walls and carved chimney piece. Notice the date, 1570, with the names of John and Ales (as Alice was spelt then) Rashleigh. John Rashleigh, who built this inn in 1570, was the son of a privateer. He maintained the family tradition by sailing in his ship, 'Frances of Fowey', with his cousins Sir Frances Drake and Sir Walter Raleigh.

The inn also boasts a stained glass window in the dining room. Bar snacks and real ale are available, while there is a family room. Opening hours are 11 am to 11 pm on weekdays, noon to 3 pm and 7 pm to 10.30 pm on Sundays.

Fowey (pronounced 'Foy' as in 'Joy')

The place name refers to a beech tree. The port is beside the River Fowey, which rises near Brown Willy (see walk 5). The museum and an

The Ship Inn, Fowey

aquarium are near the Ship Inn and the Tow Quay. The parish church is also close to the pub. Dedicated to St. Fimbarrus, it may have been founded by St. Finbar on his way between Ireland and Rome in the sixth century. Fowey is at the southern end of the Saints Way, but it is better known for pirates and smugglers. Ships from here besieged Calais in 1346, while the archers sailed from here to Agincourt in 1415. Traffic was not all one way. In 1457, the French sacked Fowey. Nowadays Fowey is the ninth port in the country, going by value of cargo. This is because English China Clay exports through it. You are more likely to see the estuary full of yachts. Writers are also attracted here, with Sir Arthur Quiller describing Fowey in 'The Astonishing History of Troy Town'. Alfred Tennyson and Kenneth Grahame (author of 'Wind in the Willows') visited him here.

Readymoney Cove

No, you won't need to pay a toll here! The name comes from the Cornish for 'stony ford'. The mock castle used to be a limekiln.

St. Catherine's Point

Here was another of the coastal chapels dedicated to St. Catherine. Its strategic location led Henry VIII to build a castle here in 1540.

Polridmouth

This cove is where Rebecca was murdered in the novel of that name by Daphne du Maurier. In real life, the Belgian coaster 'Romanie' was wrecked here in January, 1930. The red and white striped Daymark on the Gribbin is 84 feet high and was erected in 1832. This is an ancient beacon site, used to warn of the Armada in 1588.

Menabilly

Daphne du Maurier trespassed in its grounds before arranging a lease here. Such was its power to inspire her. The novelist lived with her family in the old Rashleigh family estate from 1943, moving in when her husband was serving in the war, until 1967, after her husband's death. Menabilly was 'Manderley' in 'Rebecca'.

Fowey Quay

The Tristan Stone

'DRVSTANS HIC IACIT CVNOWORI FILIVS' are the words inscribed on this sixth century stone. (Most books print this as DRUSTANUS HIC IACIT CUNOMORI FILIUS)

It originally stood near Castle Dore, about two miles north of here. This seven feet tall grave stone is an exciting survivor from the days of King Arthur. It brings to life the legend of Tristan and Iseult, or Isoude. The inscription translates as *'Tristan the son of Cunomorus lies here'*. Cunomorus was a King of Dumnonia, as Cornwall then was, while he was also known as Mark. Mark was Tristan's uncle in the legend but this may have been a change caused by the need for propriety (medieval French-speaking courts caused Merddyn to become Merlin to avoid an association with the French swear word, so a son would probably become a nephew in delicate circumstances).

Briefly, Tristan escorts Iseult from Ireland to marry Mark (his uncle or father). They drink the love potion intended for Mark and his bride on their wedding night. Bound in eternal love, they meet secretly and are finally united in death. Nearby Castle Dore was occupied in Arthurian times and may have been King Mark's Citadel.

The Walk

1. Go right up Lostwithiel Street. Turn left along the Esplanade. Pass the Old Grammar School Garden, then the ferry to Polruan on your left. Continue along a No Through Road ahead, keeping above the estuary on your left. Fork left down to the cove at Readymoney.

2. Continue up a lane which soon deteriorates to a path. Reach a National Trust sign for 'Love Lane Footpath to Lawhyre' at the edge of Covington Woods. Turn sharply left along a shaded path. Bear left at a fork marked by another National Trust sign. Emerge at St Catherine's Point. Follow the Coast Path, keeping the sea on your left. Take the middle path ahead through woodland and continue through a kissing gate to Allday's Fields.

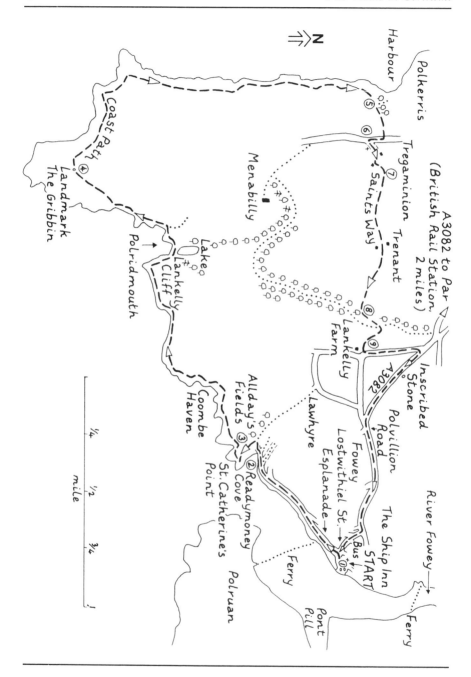

3. Go ahead along the Coast Path, keeping the sea on your left. Pass Coombe Haven, around Lankelly Cliffs and skirt the beaches at Polridmouth. Go straight uphill to the beacon tower on the Gribbin.

4. Continue along the Coast Path, above the sea on your left. The view encompasses Dodman Point, Mevagissey and the 'China Clay Alps' near St Austell. When you are above Polkerris Harbour, turn inland over a stile in the corner of the field.

5. Ignore a tempting path which descends to Polkerris through the wood on your left. Go ahead, inland, to a road. Turn right up it for 200 yards.

6. When you are near Tregaminion Chapel, turn left down a rough access lane to Tregaminion Farm. Go right to the farmyard, then turn left, as waymarked. Take a field gate beside a signpost (for the Saints Way), and go down to a stile beside another signpost opposite.

7. Bear right across a field. Look right for a view of Menabilly in the trees nearly a mile to the south of here. Cross the footbridge over a brook. Go ahead in the next field beside a wall on your right. Continue over a stile, pass Trenant on your left, go ahead over another stile and walk with a hedge on your left.

8. Cross the stone step stile in the corner. Bear left with a woodland path. Go under a bridge (built to carry a private road), over a stile and step across a stream. Bear right with the path, then go left with it to take a field gate and gain access to a lane.

9. Go left up the lane. Reach the A3082 road and turn right along its grassy verge. Pass the Tristan Stone on your left. Enter Fowey along Polvillion Road. Go down Lostwithiel Street to return to the Ship Inn.

12. West Looe

Route: West Looe – Coast Path – Talland – Tencreek – West Looe.

Distance: $5^1/_2$ miles.

Map: O.S. Pathfinder 1355 Looe.

Start: The Jolly Sailor, West Looe (Grid Reference: SX253532).

Access: Looe is the southern terminus of the delightful Looe Valley Line from Liskeard. This scenic branch of British Rail shouldn't be missed. If you are driving, leave the car at Liskeard Station and purchase an inclusive park and ride ticket (for one car and up to five passengers). This avoids having to park in Looe. There are also buses to Looe from Plymouth (daily, No. 72 and 273) and Polperro (daily, Nos 72, 273 and 279).

The Jolly Sailor (01503 263387)

Smugglers used to drink here as long ago as the 15th century. It also witnessed the Civil War, when the regulars were on Cromwell's side. Not surprisingly, it is full of ghosts. One may be of a man whose skeleton was discovered by accident below the spot now marked by a hook attached to an oak beam of the low ceiling by a spike. The skeleton was quickly reburied and may well still be under your feet as you drink. It is believed to be the remains of a missing account collector. The main beam in the ceiling is from the shipwrecked H.M.S. Indefatigable, from Nelson's fleet. Real ale and food are served, while accommodation should be available. Opening hours are 11 am to 11 pm on weekdays, noon to 3 pm and 7 pm to 10.30 pm on Sundays.

West Looe

In the 13th century East and West Looe were treated as separate towns with their own royal charters. They were important ports and notorious for smugglers. Mackerel fishing is still important, but the tourist industry has taken over in prime importance since steam trains reached Looe in 1860.

This conventional railway followed a canal and began as a horse-drawn mineral line. The original route from the mines at Caradon Hill opened in 1844 but it was closed north of Liskeard in 1916. Looe Island is now also known as St. George's Island. This is an understandable mistake. It should be called after St. Michael, as it was when monks lived and prayed here in the 12th century. Both saints are dragon-slayers and places dedicated to either of them have the same significance.

Two sisters live there today. Happily, they weren't there during the second world war, when German bombers mistook it for a battleship, or in the 1930s when a whale came aground and ended up being exploded.

Two thousand years ago, according to Cornish tradition, Joseph of Arimathea brought his nephew Jesus to Looe Island, Looe and Talland. Identified with Yesu, the expected saviour of the druids, this tradition helps to explain the missing years of the Jesus who returns to the Bible story 'not yet 50' (Jesus was probably born in 12 BC and crucified in 37 AD).

The cliffs overlooking Hore Stone were saved from developers when Miss Angela Brazil, the author of school stories for girls, bought them in 1922. They were bequeathed to the National Trust in 1948. The landmark above Talland is used to measure a nautical mile. It is paired with a lower one, while two more landmarks are one mile east above Hannafore. Speed trails are held for ships in the sea near here.

Looe Harbour

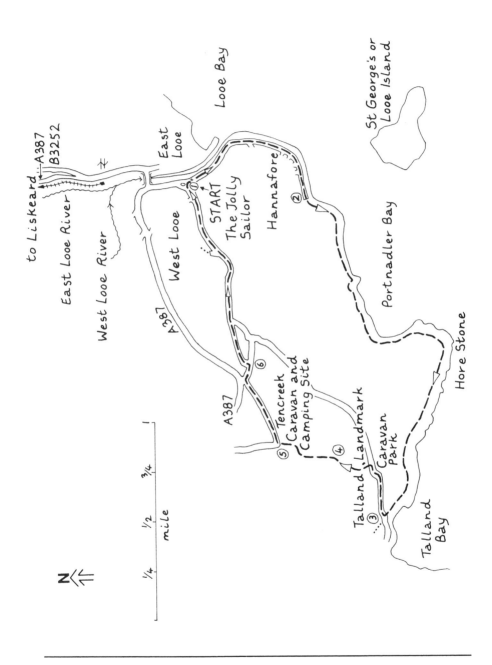

The Walk

1. Go right to the harbour and turn right to pass St. Nicholas' Church on your left. Go up Hannafore Road to its end.

2. Go ahead along the Coast Path, with the sea and Looe Island on your left. Navigation is made easy by the well maintained state of this extremely popular path. Notice how the stiles have access holes for dogs!

3. Turn right up the lane and pass through Talland. Look out for a steep wooden staircase on your left. Turn left up it to enter a field. Bear left to pass the Landmark on your right, then bear right uphill to the right hand of a pair of fieldgates.

4. Go ahead beside a hedge on your left. The path soon bears right to reach a stile in the top right corner of this field. Cross into a caravan and camping site and go left, as waymarked. Follow a hedge on your left to a stile in the corner, which gives access to a lane.

5. Turn right along the lane, soon passing the entrance to Tencreek Camping and Caravan Park on your right. Approach the A387 but turn right along a lane away from it.

6. Turn left at a junction to follow a lane signed as 'unsuitable for heavy goods vehicles'. It soon turns right. Follow it all the way, passing Downs Lane on your left and going down West Looe Hill back to the Jolly Sailor.

13. *Mount Edgcumbe*

Route: Cremyll – Formal Gardens – Thomson's Seat – Coast Path – Picklecombe Seat – Maker Church – St. Julian's Well – Mount Edgcumbe House – Cremyll.

Distance: 5 miles.

Map: O.S. Pathfinder 1356 (Plymouth).

Start: The Edgcumbe Arms, Cremyll (Grid Reference: SX454534).

Access: Come here by ferry from Plymouth. This is an ancient crossing and leaves the Devon shore about one mile from Plymouth's British Rail station. If you have invested in an excellent British Rail Cornish Rail Rover (£25 for 7 days in 1992), note that this includes Plymouth as well as all lines in Cornwall. Cremyll also has a weekday bus service (No. 73) from Cawsand.

The Edgcumbe Arms (01752 822294)

Many pubs have a ghost. Inquiries usually reveal a story based on second-hand information. Not so here. Ask the landlady about Fred the Ghost. She has seen him twice and felt his presence at other times. A very old, wrinkled man, he wears a cloak and a hat similar to the one worn by Guy Fawkes and now on display in Oxford's Ashmolean Museum. Try bed and breakfast here, although Fred seems to prefer the kitchens to the bedrooms.

The pub dates from about 1730, shortly after the Earl and Countess of Edgcumbe moved the ferry's landing stage from Barn Pool. The building may have existed as cottages before then. The first floor probably used to serve as a courthouse. It was the H.Q. of Devonport Destroyer Squadron in the second world war and has also played host to such famous sailors as Sir Francis Chichester and Sir Alec Rose. Real ale is hand-pumped, while bar snacks are available. There are tables at the water's edge and the opening hours are 11 am to 11 pm on weekdays, noon to 3 pm and 7 pm to 10.30 pm on Sundays.

The Edgcumbe Arms

Mount Edgcumbe Country Park

Poets have waxed lyrical about this place. David Garrick wrote in the 18th century:

> 'This Mount all the Mounts
> of Great Britain surpasses,
> 'Tis the haunt of the Muses,
> the Mount of Parnassus'.

Sir Richard Edgcumbe, Comptroller of King Henry VIII's household, built a Tudor Mansion here in about 1550. It was destroyed by a German fire bomb in 1941, shortly after their son and heir was killed in the same war. Bravely, Lord Edgcumbe rebuilt the house, by 1952. The estate was then purchased by Plymouth City Council and Cornwall County Council in 1971 and opened as a country park. It has a landscape reflecting 400 years of development and Gardens which enjoy a favourable climate. The trees around the shoreline were cut down when there was a threat of invasion by the French in the late 18th century, but replacements have been planted and there are nearly 200 different species of tree.

Information is available at the Cremyll Lodge Visitor Centre. Head for the Orangery (where refreshments are served), then explore the Formal Gardens. These have international themes – Italian, French, English, Amercian and New Zealand. Emerge overlooking Plymouth Sound at Thomson's Seat. An extract from 'Seasons' by James Thomson is carved on its interior wall:

'On either hand,
Like a long wintry forest, groves of masts
Shot up their spires; the bellying sheet between
Possess'd the breezy void; the sooty hulk
Steer'd sluggish on; the splendid barge along
Row'd, regular, to harmony' around
The boat, light skimming stretched its oary wings,
While deep the various voice of fervent toil
From bank to bank increased; whence ribbed with oak,
To bear the British thunder, black and bold,
The roaring vessel rushed into the main.'

This is a strategic spot for watching the ships sail from Devonport and Plymouth. Pass a blockhouse first built to defend it in 1540. A battery with a captured French eight pound cannon serves as an excellent viewing platform. The beach at Barnpool is now popular with sunbathers but in June, 1944, it was where tanks embarked for the invasion of northern France.

Pass a grotto, then a natural amphitheatre which now has a duck pond. The next 18th century embellishment is known as Milton's Temple, because an appropriate extract from 'Paradise Lost' can be read on its wall. Built in about 1755, its four ionic pillars support a small dome.

Next, the Coast Path passes a folly (a mock ruin built in about 1747) upon the slope on your right. More serious was Picklecombe Fort down on your left, built when the French were still feared in 1848. The waymarked Coast Path is now on the Earl's Drive, laid out by the first Lord Edgcumbe (1688-1758).

Turning inland to Maker Church, this has nothing to do with a St. Macra, invented in the 19th century. The name means 'ruin' in Cornish. The Cornish also called this place 'Egloshayle' (the church on the estuary). It has been in Saxon hands since the eighth century, however.

Come by ferry from Plymouth

The church, which was rebuilt in the 15th century and first recorded in 1121, is dedicated to St. Mary and St. Julian. St. Julian is the patron saint of ferrymen. A Celtic saint, probably named Sulian (a follower of St. Samson) came here in the sixth century, however. The nearby holy well is also called St. Julian's. The church has an interesting history, with its tower being used to pass semaphore messages by the Admiralty in the 18th century and a Lady Edgcumbe being found alive in her coffin at her own funeral service. Mount Edgcumbe House is open from April to October, Wednesdays to Sundays (plus Bank Holidays) between 11 am and 5.30 pm.

The Walk

1. Go right from the pub to pass the ferry on your left. Take the signposted Coast Path into Mount Edgcumbe Country Park. Cremyll Lodge Visitor Centre is on your right. Go left to the Orangery, then divert from the Coast Path to visit the Formal Gardens (including a geyser in the New Zealand part). Emerge overlooking Plymouth Sound at Thomson's Seat.

2. Go right along the Coast Path, between the Battery and the Blockhouse. Continue past a grotto, the duck pond in the amphitheatre and Milton's Temple. A shady, woodland path leads to a gate in the high fence to keep in the deer (kept here since 1539). The Folly can now be seen on your right, before you follow the waymarked Coast Path through trees down to the shoreline and back up through the trees on the safe, waymarked, path to the Earl's Drive. Continue under an arch.

3. Pass above the old jetty at Picklecombe Point. Pass Picklecombe Seat on your right. Continue along the Earl's Drive through trees.

4. Fork right from the Coast Path to take a higher track. Go through a fieldgate and follow the sinuous track to Maker Church, on your left.

5. Cross the lane to take a signposted path away from the church towards Empacombe and Cremyll Ferry. Descend a grassy slope to a little gate which leads to a road. Turn right along the road and come to a roadside trough on your right. Climb the steps behind it to the covered holy well which feeds it.

6. Take the stile next to the holy well and climb to a track. Go left, beside a fence on your right. Ignore a grassy track forking downhill on your left, but do admire the view up the Tamar, including Devonports's docks. Bear right when the fence ends, then drop down to a stile in a corner formed by the fence on your left.

7. Cross the stile and turn left through a gate in the deer fence. Descend along a track through the trees. The final section is a concrete lane, made by the American forces in the second world war. Reach the entrance to Mount Edgcumbe House on your right.

8. Go down the drive which becomes a tree lined avenue approaching Cremyll Lodge Visitor Centre, now on your left. Retrace your steps to the pub.

Above Hooe Lake Valley, Mount Edgcumbe

14. St Agnes

Route: St Agnes – St Agnes Beacon – St Agnes Head – Coast Path – Trevaunance Cove – St Agnes

Distance: 5 miles

Map: O.S. Pathfinder 1352 Perranporth

Start: Railway Inn (Grid Reference SW 720504)

Access: Buses converge on St Agnes from all directions. The No. 57 passes through on its way between St Ives and Newquay, the No. 43 comes from Camborne via Redruth, while the No. 305 provides a link with Truro.

Railway Inn (01872 552310)

Come here on a Thursday night to enjoy live music. Come anytime to see one of the finest collections of original horse brasses in the country. There are also the shoes of Lillian Board and Tommy Cooper.

The connection with shoes and horses goes back to the 17th Century, when this was a smithy. The original pub was called The Smith's Arms. This was grandly renamed The Smith's Arms and Railway Hotel in 1904, when the railway reached just a mile to the south of St Agnes. The old station has been attractively restored as an industrial unit after suffering the closure of its line in 1963.

The Great Western Railway built the line from Blackwater Junction, west of Chacewater station, to Perranporth in 1903, then extended it to Shepherds in 1905 to connect with the existing mineral line and form a through route to Newquay. Needless to say, the line was popular with holiday-makers but fell to Dr Beeching's thoughtless axe.

The real story of this place is of Anne Dorcas. She jumped into the mine shaft near the back of the pub after the death of her fiance. Her ghost once saved a young miner by enticing him away from his place

The Railway Inn, St Agnes

underground, whereupon the roof caved in! Her ghost has also been seen in this pub and is reported to be friendly, so perhaps she found her lost lover on the other side. You can stay overnight here if you wish to make contact with her yourself. Real ale and food are available, while the opening hours are 11 am to 11 pm on weekdays, noon to 3 pm and 7 pm to 10.30 pm on Sundays.

St Agnes

Or should it be St Ann? St Agnes was a fourth century Roman martyr, while Anne, or Ann, was British or Irish and beacon hills were often named after her. St Ann is easily confused with the Welsh word for fire, 'tan'. St Agnes is credited with attracting the attention of the giant Bolster, however. She tricked him into bleeding to death, which seems rather unchristian of her – but then the giant was already married.

Her church was struck by a fireball in 1905, which may be an example of an 'earthlight', as so often seen in rich mining areas. This is one of the richest, with high quality tin in abundance. Polberro Mine was worked

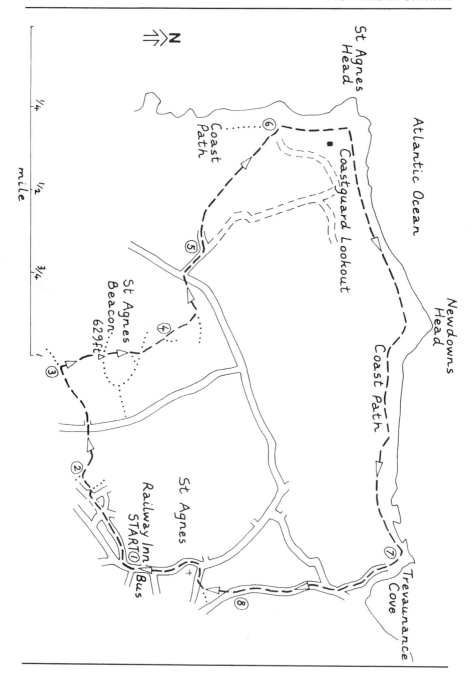

from the 16th century right up to 1941. The Miners' and Mechanics' Institute (built 1893) is a reminder that this is a mining village, despite the proximity of the St Agnes Leisure Park (with scale models of Cornish places). Winston Graham made this place the model for his St Ann, as described in his 'Poldark' books.

The Walk

1. Go right and turn right up Polbreen Lane. Go ahead at a road junction, up Whitworth Close. This begins as a lane but is joined by a road coming from your right. Pass a grass area complete with a wooden seat on your right. Opposite bungalow no. 7, turn right, then follow the footpath on your left at a waymark post.

2. Turn right at a junction with a broader path. Follow it as it bends left to a road. Cross this and take the access track to Beacon Farm and Mews Cattery ahead. Pass a row of terraced cottages on your left. Take the old green lane ahead. Emerge over a stile beside a field gate. Maintain your direction across a field, walking parallel to a hedge on your right.

3. Go ahead over a stone stile and follow the path for 20 yards. Turn right up a very narrow path which climbs through the heather to the trig point on St Agnes Beacon (with its excellent views on a clear day). Go ahead along the path over the plateau. Bear left at a fork, go ahead at a crosspaths and bear left at another fork. Pass an ancient cairn on your right.

4. Note the rocks off St Agnes Head ahead. Descend to a path junction and go left. Go down to a road at a National Trust sign. Cross the road and take the lane opposite.

5. Turn left through a gate to follow a private road but public path. When this road ends, go ahead along the footpath beside a fence on your left. When the fence ends, strike out across scrubland to the Coast Path (passing a coastal car park on your right).

6. Turn right along the Coast Path, above the sea on your left. N.B. This is the path below the metalled lane which veers right! Pass a Coast

Guard Look-out on your right, overlooking St Agnes Head on your left. Pass the National Trust's sign for Newdowns Head.

7. Reach a lane above Trevaunance Cove. Go inland along this, passing the cove on your left.

8. Bear right up a track which climbs to another road. Go right to St Agnes Church and bear left past St Agnes Hotel, on your right. Go ahead to return to the Railway Inn, on your right.

15. *Truro*

Route: Truro – Malpas – St. Clement – Pencalenick – Truro.

Distance: 8 miles.

Map: O.S. Pathfinder 1360 (Truro).

Start: The famous Old Globe Inn, Truro (Grid Reference: SW823449).

Access: The pub is in Frances Street, between the cathedral and Truro's British Rail Station. The bus station is on the other side of the cathedral, while cars will have to be parked in one of the town's signed car parks. Truro is easy to reach by train, being on the mainline between Penzance, Plymouth and London Paddington. There are also trains from Falmouth. Lots of local buses radiate from Truro.

The Famous Old Globe Inn (01872 73869)

A former landlord, called 'Essey', was a real character here until about 1970, when he died aged about 70. A singer, he once sang a solo at Westminster Abbey. Now he is a ghost, knocking plants over, switching on lights and smashing glasses. If you are sceptical, just ask the landlord and his staff. They have seen the ghost several times. Real ale and food are available in this old pub, founded in 1742. Opening hours are 11 am to 11 pm on weekdays, noon to 3 pm and 7 pm to 10.30 pm on Sundays.

Truro Cathedral

Truro

The first Anglican cathedral to be built in England for 800 years, since St. Paul's, was completed here in 1910. The foundation stone had been laid in 1880 and it incorporates part of the old medieval parish church of St. Mary's. One of the stained glass windows depicts John Wesley preaching at Gwennap Pit.

Malpas

The Malpas ferry used to be a major route from the east into Truro. Horse-drawn vehicles were carried as well as foot passengers. Legend state that Tristan and Isoude (Iseult) used this ferry in the sixth century. Malpas is French for bad passage, referring perhaps to their tragic love affair. Another appropriate explanation is the treacherous nature of the strong river currents here, especially when stormy weather forces the wind to funnel up the estuary.

St. Clement

This church dates from about 1300. That's one thousand years later than the standing stone, now near its porch, was inscribed in Latin and Ogham as the gravestone of Igniocus Vitalis, son of Torricus. A fort used to protect the ferry-crossing where the permissive footpath known as Denas Road leads through the woodland between Malpas and St. Clement. Denas is Cornish for 'fort'. It was destroyed in the 12th century during the civil war between Stephen and Matilda.

The Walk

1. Go left to pass the Royal Cornwall Museum on your left. Bear left at Victoria Square and up Boscawen Street. Divert left up Cathedral Lane if you wish to visit Truro Cathedral. Continue this route by passing the Tourist Information centre in the City Hall on your right.

2. Fork right up Prince's Street, continue along Quay Street and turn left at a dual carriageway (the A39). Go down steps on your left to take the subway under the A39. Go left up steps on the other side and pass BBC

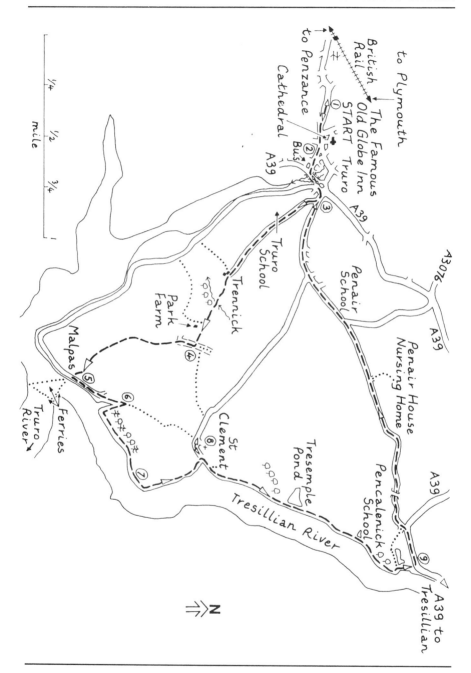

Radio Cornwall at Phoenix Wharf. Pass Malpas Road on your right, ignore the roundabout on your left and turn right at St. Clement's Hill.

3. Turn right up Trennick Lane, soon passing Truro School (an independent school founded by the Methodist Church in 1880). When the lane ends, ignore a concrete access road to a farm on your right. Go ahead down a rough track with a hedge on your left and the wall of the farm on your right. Continue along a hedged path which acquires the characteristic of an old sunken lane. Descend to cross a footbridge over a stream, follow the old green lane uphill and pass a signposted footpath on your right.

4. Turn right along a metalled lane. Pass the entrance to Park Farm House on your right. Go ahead through a gate and follow a track which deteriorates after a second gate across it to become a hedged path. Descend to Malpas, near the ferry.

5. Turn left along the road above the Tresillian River on your right. When the road bears left, uphill, go right downhill along a private road which is also a public footpath. It continues as a narrow, enclosed, path. Go through a kissing gate into woodland. Don't go through the gate beside a signpost at the far end of the wood!

Overlooking the Tresillian River, near Malpas

6. Turn right along Denas Road, the signposted permitted path (walk at your own risk!) which keeps inside the woodland. Cross a stile above this path and continue beside a fence on your right. Follow the splendid, waymarked, woodland walk above the Tresillian River on your right. Emerge over a wooden step stile and cross the foot of a field to a ladder stile.

7. Continue along the foot of the field to a stile. Go ahead over it to follow the woodland path above the river on your right. Reach St. Clement and divert left to visit the church and the ancient Ignioc Stone, now standing near the church porch.

8. Return to the riverside and go left along the private road but public footpath (soon deteriorating to a track) beside the river on your right. Pass Tresemple Pond on your left. When the shady track bends left, turn right across a footbridge on your right. Follow the path to the A39 road.

9. Turn left for 300 yards, pass a bus shelter on your left, then turn left along a lane signposted for Pencalenick. Pass the access lane to Pencalenick School on your left. Go under an arch, then pass the access drive to Penair House Nursing Home on your right. Pass Penair School on your right. Follow the pavement back to the roundabout at the edge of Truro. Retrace your steps to the pub.

16. Mevagissey

Route: Mevagissey – Portmellon – Bodrugan's Leap – Gorran Haven – Gorran Churchtown – Galowras Mill – Penwarne – Mevagissey

Distance: 7 miles

Map: O.S. Pathfinder 1361 (Mevagissey and Tregony)

Start: The Ship Inn, Mevagissey (Grid Reference SX 015448)

Access: Mevagissey is at the end of the B3273 road from St Austell. This place is not made for cars, so come here on the frequent daily bus service, No. 26 from St Austell, where there is the nearest railway station. The bus stops outside the Ship Inn.

The Ship Inn (01726 843324)

Lil Barron was the landlady here from 1910 to 1947. You may sit next to her, however. If she vanishes, or can't be seen by your partner, compare the ghost's likeness with a photo of Lil kept near the bar. She was last seen by a customer in October, 1991. This pub used to be famous for the ghost of a young, weeping, lady. She hasn't appeared lately, but if you stay overnight in Room No. 2 (bed and breakfast is avail-able) you may see the ghost of a naval captain. He likes to pull the bedclothes off young ladies, such as the landlord's daughter, at night. Real ale and food are available to fortify you for the night. The opening hours are 11 am to 11 pm on weekdays, noon to 3 pm and 7 pm to 10.30 pm on Sundays. This inn dates from the 17th century.

Mevagissey

Pilchards used to be landed by the million here. Some fishing, for a variety of species, carries on. Smuggling was the other mainstay of the village whose name is a combination of the Celtic Saints Meva and Issey. Tourists are the main business now and there is a magnificent Model Railway exhibition to entertain them.

Bodrugan's Leap

Nearby Chapel Point is said to have had a chapel (and a beacon) from which Tristan jumped to escape from King Mark. If he did he presaged an event at nearby Turbot Point nearly one thousand years later. Sir Henry Bodrugan, a supporter of Richard III, was chased here by Sir Richard Edgcumbe after Henry VII gained the throne. Sir Henry rode his horse over this cliff and may have escaped in a waiting boat to France.

Gorran

The early sixth century St Goronus (or Guron) came here from Bodmin.

Galowras Mill

This may have been a tidal mill, before the estuary silted up. Some think it is behind the name of Portmellon, but 'Mellon' also sounds like the Cornish for yellow making the place-name 'Yellow Cove'.

Penwarne

This was the home of 'One-handed Carew', who lost a hand to a cannon-ball at the siege of Ostend in 1601.

The Walk

1. Go right along Fore Street. Turn left at Jetty Street to visit the harbour. Go right and turn right up an alley back to Fore Street. This becomes Polkirt Hill and climbs to give a good view of Mevagissey and its harbour on your left. Follow the road to Portmellon.

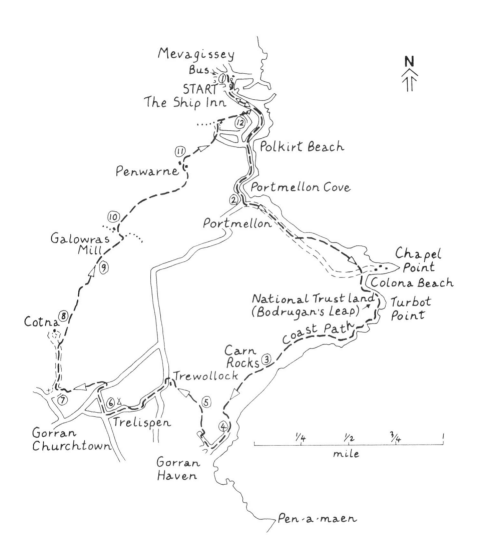

Mevagissey
Bus
START
The Ship Inn

①

⑫

Polkirt Beach

⑪
Penwarne

Portmellon Cove

②

⑩
Galowras
Mill

Portmellon

Chapel
Point
Colona Beach

⑨

National Trust land
(Bodrugan's Leap)

Turbot
Point

⑧
Cotna

Coast Path

Carn
Rocks ③

Trewollock

⑦

⑥ x

⑤

Trelispen

④

Gorran
Churchtown

Gorran
Haven

¼   ½   ¾ |
mile

Pen-a-maen

N
⇑
⇑

2. Turn left up Chapel Point Lane, a No Through Road which is part of the Coast Path. Reach Colona Beach, on your left. Go ahead over a stile beside a gate and enter the National Trust's land at Turbot Point which is known as Bodrugan's Leap. Turn left through a small wooden gate and walk between the sea on your left and a fence on your right.

3. Emerge over a stile and go ahead across a field inland of a prominent rock and bushes. Continue over a stile in the next corner and go ahead above the sea on your left. Climb wooden steps to a stile and follow a fenced path down to another stile. Cross it to reach a lane.

4. Go right to reach a T junction and a signpost. Turn right up Cliff Road, which is also the signposted Public Footpath to Trewollock. Take the first turning on your right. At its top, turn right along the signposted Public Footpath between houses Nos 50 and 53. This narrow path turns left past No. 50's garden, then right over an old stone stile and a new wooden stile. Go ahead across a field by what may be a temporary (single strand) wire fence on your right.

5. Reach a signpost at the corner of the hedge ahead. Turn left to walk beside the hedge on your right. Take a gate ahead to follow a hedged track. Pass farm buildings on your left, then bear left through a gate to a road. Go left, pass White Cottage on your left and follow the road as it bends right. Pass Trewollock Lane on your left. Pass Trelispen, with its craft centre and campsite.

6. Turn right along a lane marked as 'unsuitable for motors'. Turn right at a junction along another lane for 150 yards. Turn left over a stone stile and along the signposted Public Footpath to St Gorran's church. This bears left to cross the field diagonally to a stone stile near its bottom corner. Go ahead beside a hedge on your right in the next field. At its bottom, go right over stepping stones. Cross a stile and take the path to St Gorran.

7. Turn right at the No Through Road signposted as a Public Footpath to Galowras Mill. Pass St Gorran's church on your left. Look for a signpost on your left. This points to a stone stile beside a field gate on your right. Turn right off the rough lane to follow this path across a field to a stile in the hedge opposite. Bear slightly left in the next field to cross another stone stile in a hedge.

8. Bear slightly right downhill to cross a stone stile in the hedge just to the right of a field gate. Descend with a fence on your right. When you are almost at the bottom, turn right over a stile and go ahead to a gate. Follow the well-trodden path past four trees to a wooden step stile in the next hedge.

9. Go ahead through West Bodrugan Wood Nature Reserve. Pass a pool on your left. Go ahead along a woodland path. Go through the gate across it, then turn sharply left to follow a rough lane over a bridge to Galowras Mill.

10. Turn right along the signposted Public Footpath. This goes through a gate and over a slab footbridge. Bear right to follow a distinct path along the side of the valley which is on your right. Take gaps in two hedges ahead, then swing left to Penwayne. Go through the gate and follow the track past the farmhouse on your right and farm buildings on your left.

11. Follow the farm's access track to a road, go left and take the track signposted as a Public Footpath ahead, while the road bends right. Go through the field gate at the end of the track. Turn right to pass a house and a ruin on your right. Continue beside a hedge on your right and down to a metal gate. Go down steps and turn right for 20 yards passing Polhaun on your left.

12. Turn left down a signposted Public Footpath, towards the sea. Emerge at a road beside Honeycombe House. go left, downhill, back into Mevagissey.

17. St.Ives

Route: St. Ives – Coast Path – Trevega Cliff – Trevail Mill – Trevalgan – Trowan – Tinners Way – St. Ives.

Distance: 8 miles.

Maps: O.S. Pathfinder 1364 St. Ives and Penzance (north).

Start: The Sloop Inn, St. Ives (Grid Reference: SW519408).

Access: Motorcars shouldn't clog up places like St. Ives! Come by train, on the branch line from St. Erth, or by bus. There are regular daily bus services from Penzance (Nos 16 and 17), plus summer services from Hayle (weekdays, No. 14), Land's End (Sundays to Fridays, No. 15) and Newquay (daily, No. 57).

The Sloop Inn (01736 796584)

This old artist's and fisherman's inn is one of the most famous pubs in the world. The fishermen came first, presumably when the pub was founded as long ago as 1312. Artists love this place, with its clear light. Turner came in the late 19th century, followed by Whistler, Sickert, Ben Nicholson, Barbara Hepworth and Bernard Leach, the potter. Hyman Segal drew sketches for this pub, while Giles has featured it in cartoons. Artists still assemble in the bar on Wednesday evenings. During World War II this pub was, by contrast, Marine Commandos HQ. The Dieppe Raid was planned here. Meanwhile, the lifeboat may be seen sitting outside. Real ale is served, as are bar meals (including seafood provided by local fishermen). Opening hours are 11 am to 11 pm on weekdays, noon to 3 pm and 7 pm to 10.30 pm on Sundays.

St. Ives

This popular, picturesque, seaside resort could be reached by train in 1877. Since then tourism has become the major local industry, replacing fishing. There was a Bronze Age fortress on St. Ives Head (also known as

The Sloop Inn, St. Ives

The Island, because it was once a real island). This guarded the tin trade. Trade links were strong with Ireland and the female St. Ia came from there in about 500 A.D. A church and holy well are dedicated to her, while the name St. Ives is derived from St. Ia. Follow the Coast Path to Hor point. Despite St. Ives' reputation as a centre for artists, the town council saw fit to designate this part of the coast as a rubbish tip in 1957. The owner promptly sold the land to the National Trust and dared the Councillors to proceed with their plan. The return path follows a traditional 'coffin route'. The coarse grassland is rich in flora, while the hundreds of little fields reveal the prehistoric pattern of agriculture.

The Walk

1. Go left to walk past the harbour on your right. Turn left at the end to go up the old cobbled lane to the museum in Wheal Dream. Take the signposted Coast Path ahead, keeping the sea on your right. Pass behind the Coastguard Look-out.

2. Go down the railed steps towards the sea. Go left along the Coast Path, with the sea on your right. Reach Porthmeor Beach, follow the road above it, then take the Coast Path above the rocks at the end of the beach. Navigation is fairly simple. Keep the sea on your right and follow the well-trodden path. Don't expect solitude! Continue over two stiles and through a kissing gate beside a signpost. Notice a brown-painted post numbered '15' (part of the Trevalgan Farm Trail). A later Farm Trail notice points out where 'Bessemer City' was shipwrecked in 1941 (the crew were saved and the tinned food in the ship supplemented local rations for weeks). Go ahead over another stile.

3. Follow the Coast Path through a little wooden gate and walk with a fence on your left (ignore a fieldgate in it). Cross a stile (the trig. column on Trevega Cliff is a traditional landmark, but its presence cannot be guaranteed now that it has been made redundant) and descend to cross a stream by a stone footbridge.

4. Climb to a path junction and leave the Coast Path by turning sharply left. The well defined path leads inland to join a track.

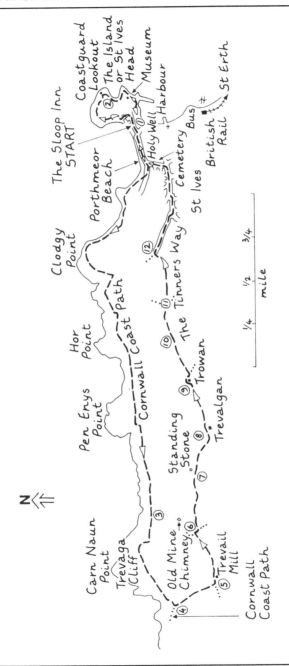

5. Turn left along the track to Trevail Mill (an old water mill, grinding corn). Go ahead along the signposted path, which is well-trodden. Reach a grassy track and ignore a gate on your right.

6. Go ahead at a crosstracks to take the signposted path between hedgerows. After 50 yards, turn left over a stile beside a signpost. Enter a field at a corner. Directions are necessarily more detailed from now on. Pay attention to the number of fields you cross! Go ahead beside a hedge on your left. Cross a stile in the corner and keep beside the hedge on your left in the second field. Cross a stile 30 yards to the right of the corner ahead. Continue past three more fields, linked by stiles in the corners.

7. Enter the sixth field and soon bear left through a gate. A standing stone is in the seventh field, on your left. Go right to cross a stile in the corner. Continue over a stile in the corner of the eighth field. Cross the ninth field to the left hand (seaward) of two fieldgates ahead.

8. Cross a stile in the corner of the 10th field to pass the buildings of Trevalgan Farm on your right. Continue over a stile into the first field after this farm. The next stile has a black and white waymark post. Go ahead over a second field. Take the stile beside a gate and bear slightly left over the third field to a stile beside another black and white waymark post. Walk with a hedge on your left in the fourth field and go ahead through a gate to the fifth field. Keep the hedge on your left and cross a stile beside a gate ahead.

9. Turn left to pass through the farmyard at Trowan. Turn right along the concrete farm track. Go through a gate to leave the farmyard and immediately turn left over a stile waymarked with a black and white waymark post. Walk beside the hedge on your left in this first field after Trowan. Continue over a stile, across a second field and over a stile beside a Tinners Way waymark post (with a black engine house emblem). Go ahead over a third field, cross a stile, a narrow fourth field and another waymarked stile.

10. Keep close to the right hand edge of the fifth field. Take the gap ahead, keep the hedge on your right and cross a waymarked stile to reach the seventh field. Walk beside the hedge on your right to a gap in the corner. Continue over a stile and follow a rutted track to join a stony track where a public footpath sign points back towards Zennor.

The Tinners Way – going back to St. Ives

11. Cross the track to cross the stile opposite. Bear slightly right to pass through a waymarked gap. Walk with a hedge on your left in the next four fields (linked by stiles). Take a hedged path downhill on your left (be careful not to take the gate into the field on your left before it). After 50 yards, turn right over a waymarked stile. Go left to follow the hedge on your left to a stile in the bottom corner. Go ahead along a narrow hedged path. Emerge at a lane.

12. Turn right along the lane to a T junction with a road. Go left and follow the road down to Porthmeor Beach. Pass St. Ia's holy well on your right. Retrace your steps back to the Sloop Inn, St. Ives.

18. Redruth Breweries

Route: Redruth – Carn Brea – Redruth

Distance: $5^1/_2$ miles

Map: O.S. Pathfinder 1359 Camborne (North)

Start: Rose Cottage Inn, Redruth (Grid Reference SW 697421)

Access: Redruth has a station on the mainline between Plymouth and Penzance. Buses stop at the railway station and come from a variety of places, including Camborne (Nos 38, 40, 41, 45, 47, 48, 49, 61 and 315), Penzance (No. 18), Truro (Nos 18, 40, 315 and 321), Helston (No. 34 and 321), Falmouth (Nos 41 and 61), St Agnes (No. 43), St Ives (No. 57) and Newquay (No. 57).

Rose Cottage Inn (01209 212129)

This is the nearest pub to Redruth Breweries, whose Cornish Original real ale is served here. It used to be the pub frequented by gypsies and still is when they gather locally each Whit Monday. There's always plenty of life about the place, with regular music and discos. Part of the pub is said to have been built over an old Celtic Church graveyard and an old granite cross has been found in the garden. The only ghost, however, is of a former landlord, called George, who has often been seen by staff and customers. Opening hours are 11 am to 3 pm and 6 pm to 11 pm on weekdays, noon to 3 pm and 7 pm to 10.30 on Sundays. Food is available.

Redruth Breweries

The old Redruth Brewery was bought by Devenish and renamed the Cornish Brewery from 1986. A management buy-out in 1991 led to its rebirth as the independent Redruth Breweries.

Rose Cottage Inn, Redruth

Redruth

This was once the centre of the Cornish mining industry. The mines at the foot of Carn Brea were particularly rich. Now, just a ruined engine house survives. The Carn Brea mines were first worked for copper, but tin became more important by 1881, when the depth reached 1710 feet and there were 29 miles of levels.

Over 1000 people were employed, making the eventual closure in 1921 a catastrophe for the local economy. By then the railway had made the tourist industry well-established. The first trains served the mines, with the West Cornwall Railway opening in 1843 and running between Redruth and the port at Hayle. It was later extended in both directions, to Penzance in 1852 and to Truro in 1853. A third rail was added in 1866 so that Brunel's broad gauge (7ft 0 $^1/_4$ins) trains could complete through journeys from London Paddington. The standard gauge of 4 ft 8.$^1/_2$ins triumphed in 1892 and the first Cornish Riviera Express ran in 1905.

The Georgian church of St Euny has a 15th century tower. The lychgate covers an extra-long coffin rest for use following major mining accidents. There is a relief bust of William Davey, who did so much to improve mining methods.

There is a link between minerals, sacred ancient sites and strange lights which have been dubbed 'Earth Lights' (see 'Earth Light Revelation' by Paul Devereux, Blandford Press, 1989). Three adults and at least 90 children at Treleigh C.P. School, Redruth, watched an 'earth light' cross the sky above Carn Brea in July, 1976.

The granite tors on Carn Brea have been worn by wind, frost and rain into marvellous forms, surrounded by a sea of purple heather and yellow gorse. The eastern end of the hill was occupied by a prehistoric fort. The locals made stone axes here in Neolithic times, while hut circles have been dated to the Iron Age.

The restaurant which flies the Cornish flag is housed in a 14th century castle. This was a hunting lodge when thick forest covered these slopes. At the Carn's highest point (some 760 ft) is a monument erected in 1836 to Lord De Dunstanville. Better known as Francis Bassett, 'The Miners Friend', this rich but benevolent mine owner was the first member of this old Cornish family to be ennobled. This big tower (90 ft high) was erected by the county. Its builder, Joseph Prior of Gwennap, made it into a tapering hexagonal column rising to a stumpy cross with a diamond lozenge.

The Walk

1. Go right along Chapel Street's pavement to pass Redruth Breweries on your left. Turn left along Little Vauxhall, then go left along the signposted public footpath. This goes under an arch and turns right. Walk with a fence (of the brewery) on your left and a wall on your right. Emerge at the road opposite Rose Cottage Inn.

2. Ignore Forth Noweth on your right, bear right up the road past Rose Cottage Inn on your left and reach a crossroads with traffic lights. Turn right along West Street. Bear left up Church Lane, which takes a tunnel under the railway. Ignore paths going left after the tunnel. Bear right to reach a road (Coach Lane).

3. Turn left to the junction with Trevingey Road. Go right along this, ignoring Trevigney Crescent on your left and Trevigney Close on your right. Pass St Euny's Church on your left.

4. Go ahead up a No Through Road at a crossroads. Ignore a right fork before a cottage. Turn sharply left along a rough track. The castle is now above on your right.

5. Fork right uphill. Take a narrow path which passes a house on your left.

6. Go right up the castle's access track. Climb to the ridge and turn sharply left along the path to the monument. The path passes this on your left. Go ahead at a crosspaths, but fork right immediately afterwards. A narrow path descends through heather and gorse to the corner of a lane at Dove Cottage.

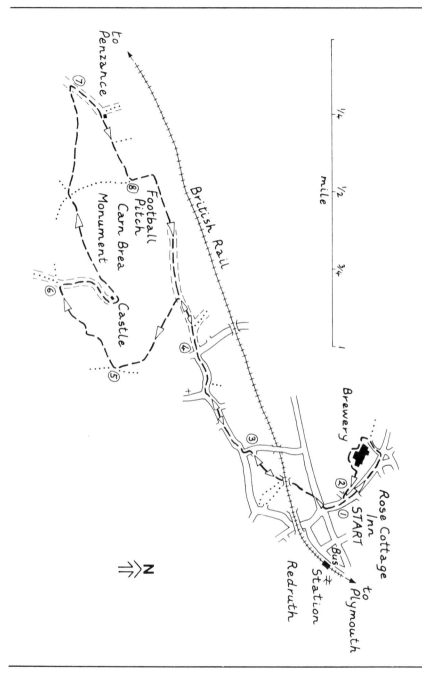

7. Turn right to walk above the cottages on your left. Ignore a lane descending on your left, then a turning going uphill on your right. Pass the next track on your left but follow the track after that to pass playing-fields on your left.

8. Turn left, then right, to pass a football pitch on your right. Go ahead along a rough lane, parallel to the railway on your left. Fork left at the point where you rejoin your outward path (which bears right). Retrace your steps into Redruth.

19. Restronguet

Route: Restronguet Passage – Halwyn – Mylor Bridge – Greatwood Quay – Restronguet Weir – Restronguet Passage.

Distance: 5 miles.

Map: O.S. Pathfinder 1366 Falmouth and St. Mawes.

Start: The Pandora Inn, Restronguet Passage (Grid Reference SW 814372).

Access: You may find it less hassle to take the train to Penryn (on the Truro – Falmouth branchline) and walk the extra two miles each way between Penryn and Mylor Bridge, where this walk can be joined at point 4. There is a good weekday bus service (No. 69) between Falmouth and Mylor Bridge. There is also an infrequent bus service (No. 322) between Helston and Truro via Mylor Bridge. There is a car park at the Pandora Inn, Restronguet Passage.

The Pandora Inn (01326 372678)

Parts of this building date back to the 13th century, when there was a farm here. By 1411, this was a pub called the Passage House. A ferry crossed Restronguet Creek from here, providing a direct link between Truro and Falmouth. Several passengers were drowned when the ferry boat sank in 1791. The inn exorcized this tragedy by changing its name to the Ship. This name didn't last long. Captain Edwards was sent in the Pandora to Tahiti to capture the mutineers of Captain Bligh's Bounty. The Pandora sank on its return trip, striking the Great Barrier Reef in 1791. Captain Edwards was court-martialled and retired to this inn. The inn was re-named The Pandora in the early 19th century.

Real ale is served here, while there is a fine restaurant. Yachtsmen can tie up here and enjoy facilities such as hot showers, fresh water supplies and public telephones. The overnight mooring fee can be reclaimed against meals in the restaurant. Bar opening hours are 11 am to 1 pm on weekdays, noon to 3 pm and 7 pm to 10.30 pm on Sundays.

The Pandora Inn, Restronguet

Restronguet Creek

The name refers to a wood on a spur of land. The silt, which can be seen in the creek at low tide, is rich in tin. Despite this, the mouth of the creek is used for oyster farming. The mouth of Mylor Creek was used as an Admiralty dockyard during the Napoleonic Wars. Ironically, the yard was used by French resistance fighters during the second world war.

Look out for exotic birds on the mud-flats.

The Walk

1. Go left and follow the path along the shore of the creek, which is on your right. This is signposted for Halwyn. This reaches a roughly-surfaced lane and bears away from the creek up it.

2. Turn left, away from Halwyn. Follow the rough access lane to the road.

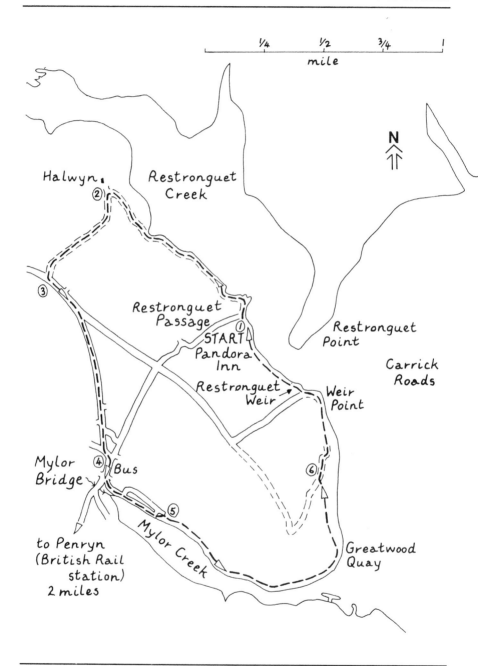

3. Turn left towards Mylor Bridge. Bear right at a fork to descend into the village. Turn left, then right to pass the Lemon Arms on your right. Reach a small clock tower on your left.

4. Bear left along Trevellan Road. Walk past Mylor creek on your right. This road is also the signposted public footpath to Greatwood and Restronguet. When the road bends left, take the narrow path ahead. Go left at a wall and bear right to a small metal gate.

5. Go ahead through the small metal gate to cross a field and take a gate in the corner back to the creekside. Turn left immediately through another gate and turn right to walk beside a hedge on your right. Follow the path above the creek on your right, although the view of it is usually obscured by a hedge. Reach Greatwood Quay and follow the path which climbs inland.

6. Reach an access lane and go right. Follow the signposted path to Restronguet, keeping the hedge on your right. Continue past Restronguet Weir and follow the path to the picturesque Pandora Inn.

20. St. Just

Route: St. Just – Youth Hostel – Bollowall Barrow – Cape Cornwall – Kenidjack Castle – Nancherrow – St. Just.

Distance: 5 miles.

Map: O.S. Pathfinder 1364 St. Ives and Penzance (North).

Start: The Kings Arms Inn, St. Just (Grid Reference: SW371314).

Access: St. Just is eight miles west of Penzance along the A3071. Cars can be parked in the square in front of the pub. There is a good bus service from Penzance (Nos. 10, 10A and 10B daily, No. 11 on weekdays only) plus a summer service from Sundays to Fridays between St. Ives and Land's End via St. Just.

The Kings Arms Inn (01736 788545)

Hicks Special Draught (HSD) is a strong real ale praised by locals here. It comes straight from wooden barrels behind the bar. These wooden barrels are made by one of only 12 surviving coopers in the country. This reflects on the integrity of the St. Austell Brewery. This was established in 1851 by Walter Hicks, who started the brewery by mortgaging his farm for £1500. The brewery is still owned and run by the family. Locally baked Cornish pasties are available, as is fresh crab whenever possible. The pub probably dates from around 1700, but the records have been lost. The former landlord witnessed the ghost of an old woman in the 1980s but she has yet to appear for the present landlord. Opening hours are 11 am to 11 pm on weekdays, noon to 3 pm and 7 pm to 10.30 pm on Sundays.

Plen-an-gwary

This circular 'amphitheatre' was used in the Middle ages to stage miracle plays and athletic competitions. Visiting Methodists later preached in it. Formerly ringed by six stone steps of benches, it may be an even older site than thought. Intriguingly, its entrance is aligned with the summer solstice sunrise.

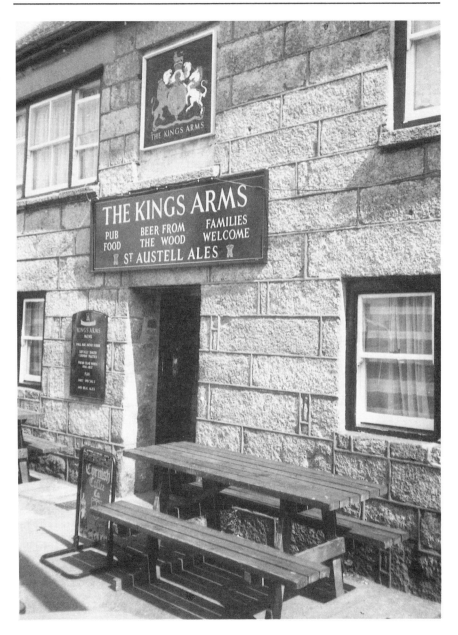

The Kings Arms, St. Just

Bollowall Barrow

This is the largest prehistoric barrow in Cornwall and a fine example of dry-stone masonry. Probably dating from the Bronze Age (1500-500 BC), it is as impressive as its inspiring setting. The nearby chimney marks the mine which provided the story of Tom Trevorrow for William Bottrell's 'Traditions and Hearthside Stories of West Cornwall' (1873). Tom was rude to the 'Knockers' (members of the fairy race – see 'Earth Lights Revelation' by Paul Devereux, 1989, for more on them) and suffered as a result.

Cape Cornwall

Climb to the chimney on the summit for a view of the Isles of Scilly on a clear day. The chimney was a ventilation shaft for Cape Cornwell Mine, which closed in 1870. A fire at the bottom forced draughts of air up the shaft, improving the circulation. The Tinners Way starts its 18 mile journey to St. Ives from here. The ramparts of an old cliff castle have now been obliterated. An early Christian site, St. Helen's Oratory, stood below an old beacon. Priest's Cove sheltered the fishing boats of miners who spent any spare time supplementing their diet. The name is derived from Porth Just. Just was pronounced 'Jeest', as in Welsh, while Porth meant port. The name was eventually distorted to Priest's.

Kenidjack Cliff Castle

Stone Age tools were made here, then tin and copper were made into bronze. The easily accessible deposits of alluvial ore were guarded by a cliff castle. Copper was made more durable by the addition of a little tin at a melting point much lower than was needed for iron, hence the Bronze Age preceded the Iron Age.

St. Just Church

Notice the Market Cross near the churchyard's southern entrance. It was returned here in 1965 after being thrown down a well in the 19th century by the Rev. Gorham, who described it as 'popish furniture'. In fact, it is a reminder of the earlier Celtic Church. Two medieval wall paintings survive inside the church. See also the gravestone of Selus, who may have been the late sixth century son, or grandson, of Gereint (a local ruler) and the brother of the Iestyn whose name was latinised into Just.

The Market Cross, St. Just Church

The Walk

1. Bear right across the square to take Market Street. Pass the Commercial Hotel and the Post Office on your left. Notice the Plen-an-gwary in a gap between houses on your right. Continue past the bus stops and car park on your left, with the fire station and library on your right.

2. Turn left to follow a road out of town, becoming 'unsuitable for motors'. Go ahead over a stone stile beside a fieldgate at the end of the road. Follow a flower-bedecked wall on your right, continue over a stile and down to a small gate. Take an enclosed path up to a lane.

3. Turn right and soon fork right (passing Land's End Youth Hostel on your left). Turn left along a shady path when the road bends right. Turn sharply right. Turn sharply right at a path junction. Cross a flat, concrete, bridge over the stream. Turn left along a road going towards the sea.

4. When you are level with the second house across the valley, bear right up a rough track. Follow this up the cliff to a road at a stone Coast Path waymark post. Divert right briefly to see Bollowall Barrow on your right.

5. Return towards the sea and go ahead along the stony track when the metalled road ends. Descend to Cape Cornwall. Turn sharply left at the bottom track junction and go down to picturesque Priest's Cove.

6. Turn right up the road past the car park on your right. Turn left with the Coast Path, walking with a wall on your right. When the path forks, go left to keep above the sea on your left. Follow the path as it bears inland above a valley.

7. Fork left at a waymark post to descend with the Coast Path to a wooden footbridge over a stream known to some as Tregeseal and others as Nancherrow Stream (Nan is similar to the Welsh 'nant', meaning stream). Reach a valley track below houses.

8. Turn left along the track until a signpost and stile on your right. Bear right over it to climb to a track at a Coast Path waymark pillar. Go left towards the sea but soon turn sharply right up the waymarked Coast

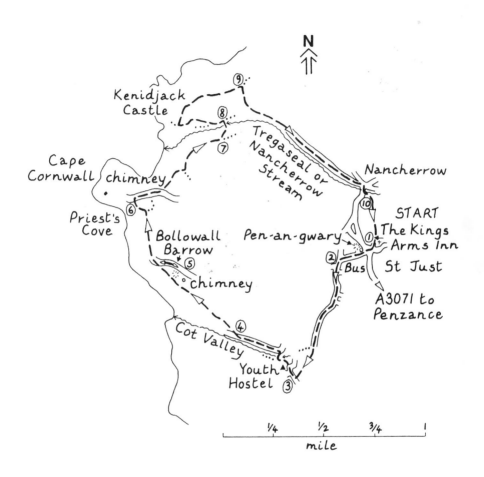

Path. Reach a ruined building on your left at the top. You may divert left here to explore the headland of Kenidjack Cliff Castle. Retrace your steps and pass the old Rifle Club butts on your right. Follow the Coast Path to a junction with a broad, stony, track.

9. Turn right along the stony track, which becomes a metalled lane as you go inland. Reach a road junction at Nancherrow and turn right over the bridge.

10. Turn left up steps near the road sign for St. Just. Follow the signposted public footpath which bears right up the field to a stile. Take the path towards St. Just church, whose tower looms ahead on the horizon. Cross three more fields and stiles to an enclosed path which leads past the church. Notice the old Market Cross near the western entrance to the churchyard and go right back to the square and the pub.

21. *Madron*

Route: Madron – Madron Well – Lanyon Quoit – Ding Dong – Boskednan – Carfury – Trythall – Madron.

Distance: $6^1/_2$ miles.

Map: O.S. Pathfinder 1364 St. Ives and Penzance (North).

Start: King William IV Inn, Madron (Grid Reference: SW454319).

Access: Madron is one mile north-west of Penzance on the B3312 road. Patrons may park at the rear of the pub, while there is usually room to park near the church. There is a bus stop near the pub for the excellent daily Hoppa D bus service from Penzance and for bus No. 11 on weekdays between St. Just and Penzance via Morvah.

King William IV Inn (01736 63022)

This homely, attractive pub dates from about 1700. Since William IV didn't reign until 1830 (preceding Queen Victoria in 1837), it must have had a different name originally. The landlady has promised to find out what it was by the time that you call. Real ale is available, while food is served from 12.30pm. The opening hours are 11 am to 3 pm and 6 pm to 11 pm on weekdays, noon to 3 pm and 7 pm to 10.30 pm on Sundays.

Madron Well

This is a mini-lourdes, with ribbons and handkerchiefs suspended from nearby branches to witness for this. They are left here for good luck. People come in search of cures, such as that found by John Trelille in 1640, which was vouched for by a bishop. Crippled since an accident when aged 16, John was told in a dream at the age of 28 that he should bathe in Madron Well or the stream running from it to receive a cure.

John lay before the altar in the chapel (or Baptistery), prayed and washed himself in the stream running from the well through the chapel.

The King William IV Inn, Madron

He slept for an hour and a half, then cried out in pain. His companions lifted him up and he found his limbs and joints were stronger. He was able to go partly erect. Crutches were provided and in a few days he could use them to walk a bit.

He returned to the chapel and did as before. He found himself stronger and was able to dispense with one crutch. The third week he awoke from sleeping in the chapel to find himself completely cured. Four years later he enlisted as a soldier. Bishop Hall of Exeter visited Madron and John Trelille and accepted that this was a true cure.

In the early 19th century An Katty made a living from showing visitors how to effect cures here. Children had to be stripped naked and plunged in the water three times 'against the sun' (west to east) then passed quickly nine times around the spring in a clockwise direction. Silence had to be observed. The water was particularly good at curing shingles and skin diseases.

The Chapel is now in ruins, having been visited by Cromwell's men. It dated from at least the 14th century, probably even from the age of the

Celtic saints, including the 6th century Maddern. Modern research is going on here, some of which has been recorded in 'Places of Power' by Paul Devereux (Blandford, 1990). If you come at night be careful not to disturb people doing research on dreams.

Lanyon Quoit

This the most famous of Cornwall's 'chambered tombs', is also the most restored. The capstone used to be high enough for a man on horse back to ride under. It also had four stone supports. Having stood for at least 5000 years, it fell a victim of vandals who dug underneath it in the early 19th century. A severe storm in 1815 made the weakened structure collapse. The locals raised the money to pay for it to be restored in 1824, using machinery. The three unbroken uprights were repositioned at a deeper level. The capstone also lost a bit in the process. Nevertheless, it is still an impressive monument which may, or may not, have originally been buried in a long barrow.

Lanyon Quoit

Ding Dong

This is reputedly the oldest mine in the country. Tin was precious in the Bronze Age about 4000 years ago. Joseph of Arimathea is said to have brought Jesus here (see 'Did Our Lord Visit Britain, as they say in Cornwall and Somerset? by Rev. C. C. Dobson, published by Covenant). The ruins belong to its last period, between 1814 and 1878, when it was one and a half miles long and three quarters of a mile wide. The deepest

The restored engine house, Greenburrow Shaft, Ding Dong Mine

shaft was 810 ft and there were 10 miles of levels covering 504 acres. All this is represented by an engine house (there were two more going east). This engine house, at Greenburrow Shaft, is a conspicuous landmark and has been restored. It dates from 1865.

The Walk

1. With your back to the pub, go right to a road junction. Turn right along Bellair Road to see Madron's 14th century parish church on your left. Turn sharply right up Church Road to pass the back of the pub on your right. Turn left at the road junction, passing Aldreath Road on your right. Pass the bus shelter and the cemetery on your left.

2. Bear right over a stone stile and walk around a field keeping beside a hedge on your right. Cross a stone stile in the corner and continue with a hedge on your right. Go ahead over another stone stile and along a hedged path. Reach a metalled lane and go right for 20 yards.

3. Turn right, as signposted, for Madron Wishing Well. Follow a hedged path to a wooded area where two paths on your left are marked by ribbons and handkerchiefs tied to the trees. These lead to a mire and a difficult to locate stone-lined well. Continue along the dry path to a notice detailing the history of Madron Well and Baptistery. Follow the path to the Baptistery, or chapel, where there is a healing spring. Retrace your steps to the lane and go right, soon passing a stone cross at the roadside on your right.

4. Bear left at a fork (away from the private road to Boswarthen Farm). Follow the hedged track to a stone stile, marked by orange paint. Cross a field to a stone stile to the left of a gate. Continue with a wall on your right. Take the stile in the recess ahead to put the wall on your left. Cross the stile in the next corner, follow the wall on your left to another stile and cross it. Walk with a wall on your right to reach a road junction.

5. Ignore the No Through Road on your extreme right, but bear right along the road to Morvah. When the road bends left, look for a stone stile on your right. Cut across a field to another stile. Continue over the access track to Pontshallow (on your right) and down to a stile in the far corner.

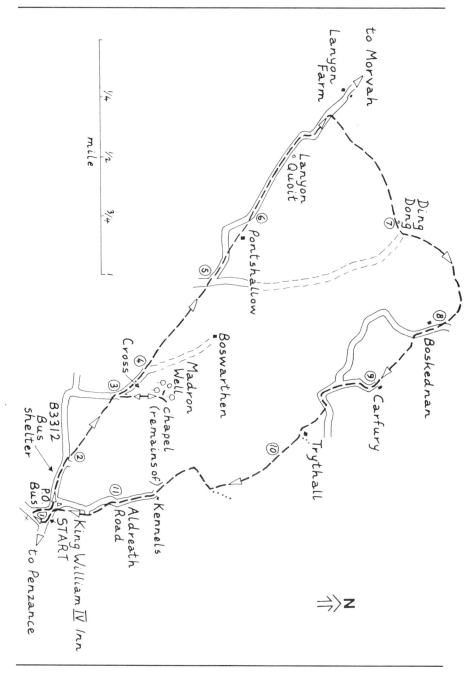

6. Turn right along the road. Visit Lanyon Quoit on your right, then follow the road around a bend on your right. About 200 yards before Lanyon Farm, turn right along a walled track. Go through a gate and walk towards the ruined engine house of Ding Dong mine.

7. Pass Ding Dong's chimney on your left. Ignore the track going right, but bear left along a rough track. This bends right to give a view across the bay to St. Michael's Mount on your right. Follow the track as it bends right to pass another old engine house on your left and Killier Cottage on your right.

8. Turn right down a lane. Pass Boskednan Farm on your right, go down the lane 150 yards and bear left through a gate into a field. Walk beside a wall on your left. Don't take the gap ahead, but do bear right, keeping beside the wall on your left. Cross a stile in the corner and go ahead over two fields to a gate giving access to a lane at Carfury.

9. Follow the lane, which bends right to pass an old chapel on your left. Descend to a road junction and go left. When this road climbs to bend left, be alert for, in 100 yards, you turn right over a stone stile. Cross a field to a gateway and walk with a wall and farm buildings on your left in the next field. Turn left through a gate to pass the old house of Trythall Farm on your left. The newer farmhouse is next. When level with it, turn right over a stile beside a fieldgate. Follow a hedge on your right.

10. Cross a stile just before a gate. Follow the hedge on your right to a stile in the corner. Continue over it and beside a hedge on your right. Cross a stile in the next corner and go ahead over an open field to its far corner, where a stile leads to a hedged track. Turn right to descend past an animal sanctuary on your right. Follow the shady track as it bends left to pass Kennels on your left. The track becomes a metalled lane (Aldreath Road). Follow it for a quarter of a mile to a bend.

11. Bear left over a signposted stone stile and walk along the fieldpath which runs parallel to the road on your right. Continue over four stiles then enter an enclosed path to emerge at the roadside in Madron. Go left to the Post Office and bus stop. Turn left to reach the King William IV pub.

22. St Michael's Mount

Route: Marazion – St Michael's Mount – Marazion – Perranuthnoe – Cudden Point – Rosudgeon – Perranuthnoe – Marazion

Distance: 9 miles

Maps: O.S. Pathfinders 1364 St Ives and Penzance (North) and 1369 Helston and Prussia Cove

Start: The Godolphin Arms, Marazion (Grid Reference SW 518306)

Access: There are plenty of buses to Marazion from Penzance (Nos 2, 12, 17, 341 and 342). Come from Helston on bus No. 2, from Camborne on bus No. 12 and from St Ives on bus No. 17.

The Godolphin Arms, Marazion (01736 710202)

Ruddles real ale is served at this establishment, which has been patronised by royalty. Conveniently situated at the start/finish of the causeway which connects St Michael's Mount with the mainland at low tide, the bar is open from 11 am to 11 pm on weekdays and from noon to 3 pm, then 7 pm to 10.30 pm on Sundays. There is a restaurant and accommodation is available.

The Fire Engine Inn, Marazion (01736 710562)

The name pre-dates the railway, having been adopted in 1780, when the pub was already 40 years old. It refers to the engine house for the local mine and is a reminder that this was originally a miners' pub. One 18th century miner, called Charlie, haunts the place and is notorious for re-arranging the furniture. Real ale and food are served, while bed and breakfast accommodation is available. Opening hours are 11 am to 3 pm and 6 pm to 11 pm on weekdays, noon to 3 pm and 7 pm to 10.30 pm on Sundays.

Ye Olde Victoria Inn, Perranuthnoe (01736 710309)

This claims to be the oldest pub in Cornwall and can point to a 12th century wall. It was erected by the masons who built the village church and provided them with accommodation and refreshments. You can stay here on a bed and breakfast basis too, while real ale and food are available. Opening hours are noon to 3 pm daily, then 6.30 pm to 11 pm on weekdays. 7 pm to 10.30 pm on Sundays. The locals will keep you talking for hours.

St Michael's Mount

Pilgrims have made their way here for centuries, perhaps for thousands of years. It is at the end (or beginning) of a long line of special places dedicated to St Michael (e.g. Glastonbury Tor). It is also our link with the continent via Mont St Michel, its counterpart in Normandy. Few places possess such a sense of magic and mystery. To the druids it was Dinsul, the city of the sun. An old Cornish name is Carreg Los En Cos, or the hoarstone in the wood. It is said that Joseph of Arimathea brought his nephew Jesus here (Marazion is also known as Market Jew, although some claim that the name is derived from the Cornish for Little Market – Marghas Vyghan). The Mount was the home of a giant, Cormoran, who was killed by Jack.

The legends have substance. A skeleton of an eight foot giant was discovered by monks in 1275. Uncovered again in 1864, it was re-buried near the altar of the chapel. The Mount is the high point nearest John

Michell's Michael or Dragon Line as it crosses Mount's Bay. This marked the line of the Beltane (May 1st) sunrise across the country and may have been marked by a chain of beacons. Miller and Broadhurst's Michael and Mary energy lines visit here, with the Mary line passing through the eastern part of the Blue Drawing Rooms (formerly the site of a Lady Chapel).

The Dairy is curiously like the Abbot's Kitchen at Glastonbury. Some great power resides here, or pulsates through. Healings (e.g. of the blind) were recorded in the 13th century, while the Archangel St Michael was seen here by fishermen in 495 A.D. Edward the Confessor encouraged the establishment of a priory by monks from the French Mont St Michel. A line drawn between the two Mounts is said to link with other such sites across Europe to reach Delos. Some say this was the Ictis that featured in the ancient tin trade. Apart from the fact that the Isle of Wight has a much better claim, this was dry land until fairly recently.

Uncharacteristically (if it were an island), the Domesday Book of 1086 does not mention the territory of St Michael's *Land* as an island, while recording an area about 30 times its present size. The great flood of 1099 may have finally drowned the submarine forest known to lie in the bay. This was, perhaps, the final remnant of Lyonesse. The Mount is the home of Lord St Levan and is in the care of the National Trust. It is open from April to October (Mondays to Fridays and most weekends) between 10.30 am and 5.45 pm.

Perranuthnoe

St Piran (whose white cross on a black background is the flag of Cornwall) came here in about 500 A.D. He taught new ways of smelting tin and replaced Michael as the Patron Saint of Cornwall. The church (Built in 1160) is dedicated to both St Piran and St Michael. The last survivor of Lyonesse (named Trevelyan) rode his horse just in advance of the waves to safety here. There is a fine view of St Michael's Mount from Trevean Cove. When workmen found a skull in a cliff here in the 19th century they were haunted by its ghost until they replaced it.

The Walk

1. Walk across the causeway, or take the ferry, to visit St Michael's Mount. Return to Marazion and go right along the pavement to eventually pass the Fire Engine Inn on your right. Continue going east.

2. Turn right with the signposted Coast Path, down a track towards the sea. Fork left along a narrow, hedged, path. Go down to the beach (obviously, do not proceed in bad weather) and go left. Climb a metal flight of stairs to the cliff top. Turn right, as waymarked. Cross a stile and walk above the sea on your right. Reach a sign marking where the Coast Path has had to be diverted (because of erosion) and turn left, inland. Walk beside a hedge on you left. Turn left with a track and follow this as it bends right to a Coast Path signpost.

3. Fork right along the signposted Coast Path. Follow a hedged path and emerge in the corner of a field. Continue beside a hedge on your left. Go ahead across the access lane to Trenow Farm Cottages and cross a waymarked stile. Continue over a field to a gap in the next hedge. Maintain your direction in the following field, keeping beside a hedge on your left. Take a stile into another field and keep the hedge on your left.

4. Go ahead over a stile in the corner. Walk beside a hedge on your left, aiming for the tower of Perranuthnoe's church. Turn left up steps in the corner to a track and turn right into Perranuthnoe.

5. Turn right along a road to the church, then turn left down through the village to bear right and pass Lynfield Cottage on your left. Turn right with the road to the cliff-top car park.

6. Turn left along the hedged lane which forms the signposted Coast Path. When the metalled lane bears left, fork right along a rough track. Fork right again and follow a hedge on your left.

7. Turn left along the signposted Coast Path (a cliff-top path above the sea on your right). Pass Trevean Cove on your right. Continue to Cudden Point.

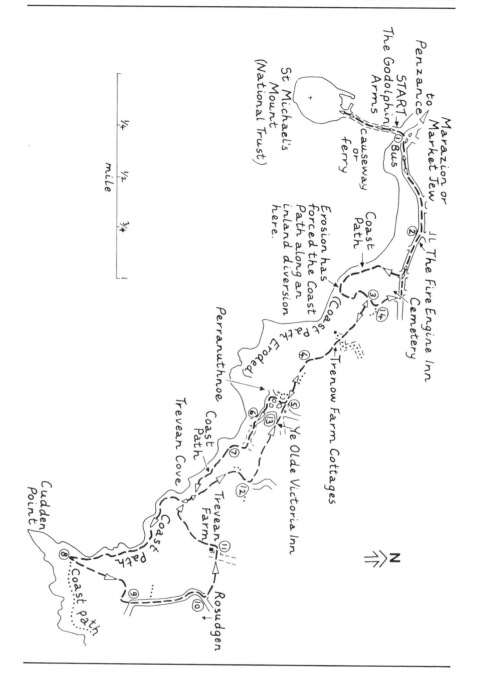

8. Turn sharply left inland. Follow the path through a kissing gate and beside a hedge on your left. Continue through a wooden gate and along an enclosed path. Reach a lane at the entrance to Prussia Cove Caravan Site.

9. Go left along the lane. Pass the first signposted Public Footpath (which crosses a stile) on your left. Follow the lane to Rosudgeon.

10. Turn left along the hedged track signposted as a Public Footpath. Cross the stile beside a gate at its end and continue beside a hedge on your left. Take the stile in the corner and follow a hedge on your right. Cross a lane to go ahead along a rough track, passing Trevean Farm on your left.

11. Go ahead along the hedged path which is signposted as a Public Footpath. Turn right as it approaches the sea. Soon turn left to rejoin your outward route (the Coast Path). Go right along it past Trevean Cove on your left. Cross a stile and fork right to the top corner of a field. Climb to a lane and go right up it to Trebarvah.

12. Turn left in the farmyard and take the signposted Public Footpath over a stile into the corner of a field. Continue with a hedge on your right and over a stile in the next corner. Cross another field, keeping the hedge on your right. An enclosed path leads to an open field. Go straight ahead to a small metal gate giving access to a lane. Go left into Perranuthnoe and Ye Olde Victoria Inn.

13. Go right from the pub to the telephone box. Turn left up a track. Cross a road to climb with the track ahead. Rejoin your outward route (at point 5) and retrace your steps along it back towards point 3. Don't forget that this involves turning left off the track over a stile into a field. You then walk with the hedge on your right, keeping it there along what is a well-trodden Coast Path diversion.

14. Having returned to point 3, turn right up a lane. This soon bears left to pass a cemetery on your left. Reach a road and go left back to Marazion and its pubs.

23. Land's End

Route: Sennen – Trevilley – Higher Bosistow – Carn Les Boel – Coast Path – Land's End – Mayon – Sennen

Distance: 6 miles

Map: O.S. Pathfinder 1368 Land's End and Newlyn.

Start: The First and Last Inn, Sennen (Grid Reference SW 357255)

Access: Buses run to the First and Last Inn, Sennen, from Penzance (Nos 1, 3 and 4) and from St Ives (No. 15). There is a good service on Sundays in the summer.

The First and Last Inn (01736 871680)

Approach this pub from Penzance and it's the Last Inn, come up from Land's End and it's the First Inn. Its history may date back to when the Phoenicians came here to trade for tin. The landlord can proudly point to a well with ancient markings. Perhaps Jesus supped here with his uncle, Joseph of Arimathea.

The church next door dates from 520 and the Irish Saint who gave his name to Sennen probably brewed mead here. The present church was built in the 13th century and this inn was used to house the masons working on it. The whole community, including the parson and the squire, were involved in enticing ships to the dangerous coast with the aid of lights at night. They swiftly stripped the wrecks of anything valuable. The squire had a tunnel from his house to the inn. Nowadays the annual influx of tourists provides the locals with financial opportunities.

This inn's special position has attracted many, including Nelson and Lady Hamilton, Diana Dors, Barbara Windsor and Ian Botham. Real ale and food are served, while there is a beer garden. Opening hours are 11 am to 3 pm and 6 pm to 11 pm on weekdays, noon to 3 pm and 7 pm to 10.30 pm on Sundays.

The View Over Lyonesse

The modern commercial exploitation of Land's End can be avoided by following this route, which just goes to show the advantage of two feet over four wheels. The Coast Path is followed along the flat-topped granite cliffs. The beach at Nanjizal almost enchanted me off the path for a swim. The water was translucent. A few hundred yards around the bay and I met a man studying the water with a pair of binoculars. The naked eye revealed a fin and a tail in the water and the binoculars confirmed that it was a basking shark ... some 300 yards from the swimmers in the bay!

The Coast Path is joined at Carn Les Boel. This is 'a very special place' to Hamish Miller and Paul Broadhurst, who describe their journey from here to the Norfolk Coast in 'The Sun and the Serpent' (1983). The Dragon line starts and finishes at Carn Les Boel, where there is a 'First and Last' standing stone. Other places on its route include Glastonbury Tor, Avebury and Royston.

On the Coast Path above Nanjizal

All eyes are on the sea, however. The Longships Lighthouse is visible, while the Seven Stones rocks which wrecked the 'Torrey Canyon' in 1976 lie 16 miles due west of Land's End. The real drama is the legend of Lyonesse, which stretched from here to include the Scilly Isles. Lyonesse was a fertile province of the ancient kingdom of Dumnonia. It boasted several towns and 140 churches.

Nigel Pennick considers the truth behind the legend in his 'Lost Lands and Sunken Cities' (1987). There is a good reason to believe that Mount's Bay was a forest around a St Michael's Mount that was once several miles inland (see Walk 22). The drowned land of Lyonesse has been encompassed by a line drawn from Land's End to the Longships Lighthouse, then for some 30 miles south-west to the Scillies and for some 50 miles from there to Lizard Point. By Roman times the Scillies were an island (Siluram Insulam).; They were recorded in the singular, however (the whole Scilly group now exceeds 140 islands).

Stone walls or hedges can be seen below high water mark in the Scillies. Romano-British brooches have been found in a stone cist on what is now the seashore. The sea between the Scillies and Land's End is only 60 feet deep. Sometime between the Romans in the fourth century and the Saxon Conquest of Dumnonia in 932, Lyonesse was overwhelmed by the sea. The cause may have been an earthquake and the traditional date is the sixth century. Only after this loss of land and change in shape did Dumnonia take the name of Kernow (Cornwall), derived from the Cornish word for a horn or promontory.

The Walk

1. Turn left down the road. Fork left to Trevescan. Reach a T-junction. Go ahead along the public footpath past Curlew Cottage to a small metal gate into a field. Continue with a wall on your right to a stile in the corner which juts out ahead. Go ahead beside a wall on your left and pass an old cross on the other side of this wall.

2. Go through the farmyard at Trevilley and bear right along a lane. Soon fork left to pass the farmhouse and buildings on your right. The lane deteriorates to a rough, grassy., track. Go ahead over a stile beside a gate and follow a wall on your right for 250 yards, then bear left to a gate near a corner of the wall ahead. Continue beside a hedge on your left. Bear left through a gap along a well-trodden path which crosses a field to a stile. Descend to the bottom of a valley. where a stone stile also serves as a footbridge across a stream which is hidden by the luxuriant vegetation.

3. Climb up to a gate in the wall above the valley. Go through it and bear right to pass a wall on your right and cross into the next field at the corner which juts out ahead and is now occupied by a plastic cattle trough. Continue beside a wall on your right. Take the gate ahead in the corner and go ahead parallel to a hedge on your right, towards Higher Bosistow.

4. Turn right along the hedged, stony, track. Pass the farm on your left and go right at a track junction. Bear left at the next fork. The hedged track ends at a gate. Go ahead over an open field to the Coast Path at Carn Les Boel.

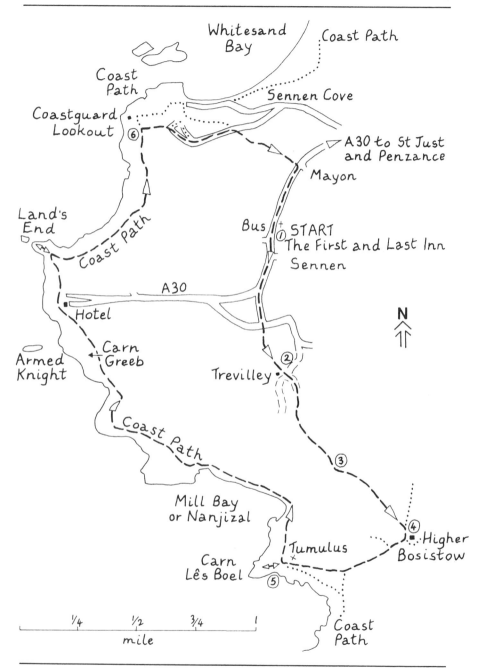

5. Go right along the Coast Path, keeping the sea on your left. Pass Land's End and continue towards an old Coastguard Look-out.

6. Turn right on an inland path which joins a metalled lane at a hairpin bend. Go right, along the upper lane. Fork left at a higher road junction. Reach a signposted Public Footpath rising from Sennen Cove on your left. Turn right to follow it inland. The narrow, metalled, path bears left. Cross a stone stile and go up steps over a wall on your right. Continue along the enclosed path which leads to the road at Mayon. Turn right back to the First and Last Inn. Pass St Sennen's Church on your left just before the pub.

24. Mousehole

Route: Mousehole – Raginnis – Kemyel Crease – Lamorna Cove – Coast Path – Mousehole

Distance: 5 miles

Map: O.S. Pathfinder 1368 Land's End and Newlyn

Start: The Ship Inn, Mousehole (Grid Reference SW469264)

Access: There is a frequent daily bus service (Hoppa A) from Penzance. There is another bus (No. 340) from Mondays to Fridays linking Penzance with Lamorna Cove via Mousehole. Buses stop at the war memorial opposite the Ship Inn.

The Ship Inn (01736 731234)

Hicks Special Draught is one of the real ales available here. Food is served, while accommodation is available. This inn dates from the 16th century and the bar is open on weekdays from 11 am to 11 pm, noon to 3 pm and 7 pm to 10.30 pm on Sundays.

Mousehole

Pronounced 'Mowzul', the name may indeed refer to a mousehole – a small local cave. In the 14th century this was the most important fishery harbour in West Cornwall. The harbour was used to import salt for the pilchard industry, while oil was extracted from the fish and exported. The old name for the port was Port Enys, with the

island (Enys) referred to being St Clement's Isle. A hermit used to live on it. Dolly Pentreath lived in Mousehole and is usually claimed as the last person to speak Cornish. She died in 1777, but John Davey of Zennor, who died in 1891, was a later Cornish speaker, while the language is being revived in local playgroups and schools, such as at the Well Being Centre, Illogan, near Redruth. Dylan Thomas and his wife, Caitlin spent their honeymoon here in 1937.

Lamorna Cove

The harbour was built to export granite (used to construct the Thames Embankment in London). In December, 1981, the cove was where the Penlee lifeboat was washed up after a double tragedy. The 'Solomon Browne' capsized while attempting to rescue the crew of the 'Union Star', a coaster on her maiden voyage. All eight of the lifeboat's crew were drowned, as were all on board the Coaster, including the Captain's wife and two teenage daughters. The public raised £3 million for the lifeboat crew's dependents.

Mousehole harbour

Penzer Point

The crew were saved when the 4068 ton steamer 'Ansgir' was wrecked here in 1920. Built in Germany, she was initially awarded to Britain as part of war reparations but had just been transferred to Japan.

Merlyn Rock

Legend states that Merlin predicted 'There shall land on the Rock of Merlin Those who shall burn Paul, Penzance and Newlyn' (an early version is found in the Cornish language). In 1595, Spanish ships did land here and go on to burn the places mentioned, as well as Mousehole. The English reprisal came at Cadiz in 1596.

The Walk

1. Go right to pass the harbour and The Lobster Pot (a hotel and restaurant) on your left. Follow the road around to the right and pass Pam's Pantry on your left. When the road bends left, go straight ahead up the narrow Cherry Garden Street. Climb steps at its end and turn left to pass Treen Villa on you left. Continue along this path (ignoring paths coming sharply from your right and forking left ahead). Climb more steps. Pass giant rhubarb. Reach Love Lane (a rough track) and cross it to take a flight of stone steps opposite.

2. Bear left up the field to a stile. Veer very slightly right in the second field to take the stile in the opposite wall. Do the same in the third field, crossing a stile to the left of a gate. Bear right across a corner of the fourth field to another stile. Cross it and turn left through the farmyard at Raginnis to reach a road.

3. Go right for just five yards, then turn left across the road and go ahead over a waymarked stile. Bear left up a long field to a waymarked stile at its end. Go ahead to follow a hedge on your right in the next field. Maintain this direction along the tops of three more fields, linked by stiles.

4. Go ahead beside the wall surmounted by a hedge on your right. Take the right of way through Kemyel Drea's farmyard. This turns right after the initial buildings, then turns left through a small wooden gate. It then crosses three wooden stiles in a narrow path between farm buildings. Emerge over a stone stile.

5. Turn left along a lane and turn right in a corner to follow a rough track. This bears slightly right at a signpost and leads between hedgerows to a stone slab footbridge. Go ahead over a stile and beside a hedge on your right to a stile beside a gate. This gives access to a rough lane. Go left along it to Kemyel Crease Farm.

6. Bear right over a signposted stone stile (just when the hedged track resumes after passing the farm buildings). Take a stile beside a gate near a recessed corner. Maintain this direction to a stile in the hedge facing you. Continue beside a hedge on your right to a stile in the corner and go ahead to Kemyel Wartha. Follow a rough track through the farmyard.

Walkers on the Coastal path between Mousehole and Lamorna

7. Fork left at a signposted path junction to take the hedged path (ignoring the signposted path across the field on your right). This path zigzags down to Lamorna Cove.

8. Turn left along the waymarked Coast Path towards Mousehole. Walk above the sea on your right to Kemyel Crease Nature Reserve. Follow the Coast Path inland, then back towards the sea. Gradually climb inland to reach a road.

9. Go right along the road. Pass Carn Du Hotel, with its Cornish flag (St Piran's Cross – a white cross on a black background) on your left. Immediately afterwards, notice a metal gate with 'Private No Admittance' on it. This is a viewpoint for Merlyn Rock, a small rock directly below (not the large St Clement's Isle to its left). Continue down the road (ignoring the track forking left). Turn right in Mousehole to the harbour. Go left back to the pub.

25. The Loe

Route: Helston – Castle Wary Mine – Degibna Wood – Carminowe
Creek – H. M. S. Anson Memorial – Loe Bar – Penrose House Stables –
Causeway – Helston.

Distance: 8 miles.

Map: O.S. Pathfinder 1369 Helston and Prussia Cove.

Start: Fitzsimmons Arms, Helston (Grid Reference: SW658274).

Access: Helston is at the junction of the A394 and the A3083. Motorists
will have to park in the street near the Fitzsimmons Arms. The bus stop
could hardly be more convenient, however. There is an excellent daily
service from Penzance (No. 2) and from Falmouth on weekdays (buses
Nos. 2 and 322). Other weekday buses include No. 33 from Camborne,
No. 34 from Redruth, Nos. 320 and 322 from Truro and Nos. 330 and 331
from Hayle.

The Fitzsimmons Arms (01326 574897)

There is handpumped real ale available at this old coaching inn, which
dates from the 16th century. Bar meals are served, while there is a beer
garden and a children's play area. Opening hours are 11 .30 am to 3 pm
and 6 pm to 11 pm on weekdays, noon to 3 pm and 7 pm to 10.30 pm on
Sundays. The pub is named after 'Battling' Bob Fitzsimmons, the local
boy who become the only Englishman to become world Heavyweight
boxing champion.

Award Winning Chips

Helston can also boast the national winners (1991) of the Daloon Fish
and Chip Shop of the Year and the Sea-fish Enterprise Award South
West 1991. Go round to Hutchinsons at 95 Meneage Street, Heltson
(01326 572679).

The Fitzsimmons Arms, Helston

Helston

This is the original 'quaint old Cornish town' of the song. Come on May 8th to see the Furry, or Flora Day (a reminder of the ancient Beltane festivities). Originally known as 'Henlan' (old sacred place), it acquired 'ton' after the Saxons reached here in the ninth century. Eventually, the name was shortened to Helston. This was a thriving port in Saxon times before the shingle bank of Loe Bar cut it off from the sea in the 13th century. Locally-produced tin was assayed, or tested, here. Edward I gave Helston the status of a stannary town. This allowed the Tinners' Courts independence. The King also named Helston as a place where tin was to be taken for coinage. The Fitzsimmons Arms stands in Coinagehall Street.

The Loe

The National Trust now owns all the land surrounding the Loe. The name is derived from the Cornish word 'logh' (meaning 'pool'). It is the largest natural freshwater lake in Cornwall and has a superb, unspoilt, setting. It formed part of the Penrose Estate until 1975 and estate tracks and roads are followed by this walk. The shingle bar which separates it from the sea dates from the 13th century. Before then, Helston was a thriving port and the Loe was the estuary of the River Cober. The shingle may come from an off-shore deposit of flint on the seabed which has been formed into a spit by both onshore and longshore drift. The silt brought down by the River Cober must be rich in tin as 30 mines operated in its catchment area in the 19th century.

Castle Wary Mine (also called Wheal Pool) is passed by this walk. The romantic Tennyson mislocated the lake where the dying Arthur's Excalibur was thrown to here. The woods are delightful, while there are plenty of birds to be seen, including mute swans, moorhens, coot, mallard, tufted duck, pochard, shoveler, teal and wigeon. The monument where the path meets the sea is to the dead from H.M.S. Anson. This 44 gun frigate was shipwrecked here in December, 1807, whilst on its way to blockade Brest. Despite the ship being beached on Loe Bar, the locals couldn't save over a hundred people from being drowned. The dead were then buried in unmarked graves on the open cliff, as was the custom, because it could not be proved that they were baptised

The old engine house, Castle Way Mine, Helston

Christians. As a result of this tragedy, a local man called Henry Trengrouse developed a rocket life-saving apparatus. The government awarded him £50, the Royal Society gave him 30 guineas and the Czar of Russia sent him a diamond ring and a silver medal. The latter had to be pawned to enable his research to continue. Trengrouse died penniless in 1854. At least Parliament changed the law to provide Christian burial for those drowned in shipwrecks.

The Walk

1. Go left down Coinagehall Street. Turn left at the bottom, down Monument Road. Go ahead at a roundabout, down the pavement of the B3304 towards Porthleven. Pass a boating lake on your right.

2. Just before a garage, fork left along the access lane to Lower Nansloe Farm. Pass the sewage works on your left. Pass the ruin of Castle Wary Mine's engine house on your right. Ignore the small wooden gate just after it. Go ahead along the concrete lane.

3. When the lane bears left to Lower Nansloe Farm bear right along a rough track. Begin by crossing a stile beside a gate, continue beside a hedge on your left and go ahead over a stile beside another gate. Follow a hedged track, bearing right over a stone stile beside a gate to reach the vast expanse of water known as the Loe.

4. Go left along the path running around the Loe, on your right. Enter woodland and keep to the path near the Loe. Turn left, with the path, away from the water. Turn right at a path junction. At the next fork, bear right to walk above the Loe.

5. Emerge from the wood through a gate. Follow the waterside path around Carminowe Creek. Bear left through a small wooden gate to join a higher track. Go right along it to pass Lower Pentire Farmhouse on your left. Follow the clear path as it bends right to cross a stream and follow the other side of the creek. Keep the water on your right to reach Loe Bar.

6. Head for the sea and the H.M.S. Anson monument, on your left. Turn right across Loe Bar and follow the Coast Path up to Bar Lodge.

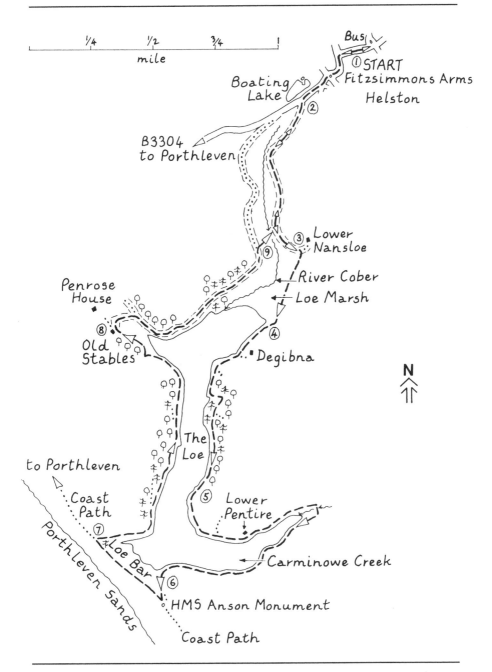

7. Turn sharply right to pass the lodge on your left. Follow the National Trust's courtesy path (open from dawn to dusk). Walk above the Loe on your right, framed by trees which shade the stony track. Reach the stable block of Penrose House.

8. Bear right along a metalled drive lined by iron railings. Turn right at a junction to follow the lane in the direction of Helston. Pass Helston Lodge and follow a stone track past the Loe on your right.

9. Turn right through a small wooden gate. Take the Causeway path, crossing Loe Marsh and the River Cober. Reach the outward route through the small gate near the old engine house of Castle Wary Mine. Turn left to retrace your steps to the pub.

26. Frenchman's Creek

Route: Manaccan – Frenchman's Creek – Helford – Dennis Head – Manaccan

Distance: $7^1/_2$ miles

Map: O.S. Pathfinder 1370 Helford River

Start: The New Inn, Manaccan (Grid Reference SW 764249)

Access: The area south of the River Helford is isolated and not very well served by public transport. If coming from Falmouth, you could use the seasonal ferry from Helford Passage to Helford Point. This runs on request between April and October. Telephone 01326 250116 or 250700 for more information. There is a bus service (No. 326) from Helston to Manaccan. This is best used on a Saturday, although the timetable also allows walkers to complete this walk (in just over three hours) on Monday and Thursday mornings.

The New Inn (01326 22323)

As is often the case, there's nothing new about this inn. It was already old when Cromwell's troops were ordered not to visit it because of its ill-reputation. Today, it serves real ale direct from the barrels. Home-made food is available, including seafood specialities. There is also a children's garden.

Opening hours are 11 am to 3 pm and 6 pm to 11 pm on weekdays, noon to 3 pm and

7 pm to 10.30 pm on Sundays. This pub has a *car park for patrons*, plus a delightful thatched roof.

Frenchman's Creek

Frenchman's Creek

The dense woodland makes this appear like an outpost of the Amazon. Known locally as Frenchman's Pill, it is a hidden, gloomy and luxuriant place. Unviolated, it has not been spoilt. The mud at low tide is picked by herons, while seaweed drapes dead trees and makes then look like a Cornish version of the Loch Ness Monster. This is a haven for all who seek peace and tranquillity.

It became a prison for Captain Bligh (of 'The Bounty') when he was mistaken for a French spy here. Arrested by the Reverend Richard Polwhele, he spent time in Manaccan's cell before the Admiralty verified his identity. The local vicars seem to have been quite enterprising. Reverend William Gregor discovered titanium (calling it Menachanite) near here, in 1790. Perhaps he was inspired by the fig tree growing out of the church, which it is taboo to prune. There may have been an obscure St Manacca, or the name may refer to the monks who settled here in Saxon times.

Smugglers were common until fairly recently and Frenchman's Pill or Creek may have acquired its name from a visiting French Ship. Sir Arthur Quiller-Couch set a short story here in 1905. Real literary fame came with the publication of Daphne du Maurier's novel, 'French Creek' in 1941. Romance and adventure immediately made this hugely popular. Daphne du Maurier had previously sailed into the creek on her honeymoon.

Literary pilgrims make their way here from all parts of the world. Down by the water's edge it is more like a mangrove swamp than the woody hiding place for La Mouette, lustful Lady Dona St Columb and her Gallic Matelot. The subsequent film had to be made in the north of California because of the Second World War (which saw the creek used by Special Services). It is hard not to agree with du Maurier about the 'strange enchantment' of this place. It is genuinely haunted, by the ghost of an old man who drowned one night when attempting to take a short cut across the creek. Tread lightly here, for you are intruders. There is a different air at Dennis Head, with its extensive coastal views. The name is derived from the ancient 'dinas'. or fort. This was fortified by the Royalists in the Civil War.

The Walk

1. Go left and turn left along the road signposted for Gweek. Pass Tregonwell Farm on your right and reach a crossroads. Go ahead, as signposted for Kestle.

2. Turn right at a T-junction to follow the No Through Road to Kestle. Turn left along the signposted Public Footpath to 'Frenchman's Pill'. This is a rough track which turns right through a gate in the wall on your right and then turns left. Descend through woodland and fork right to the famous creek.

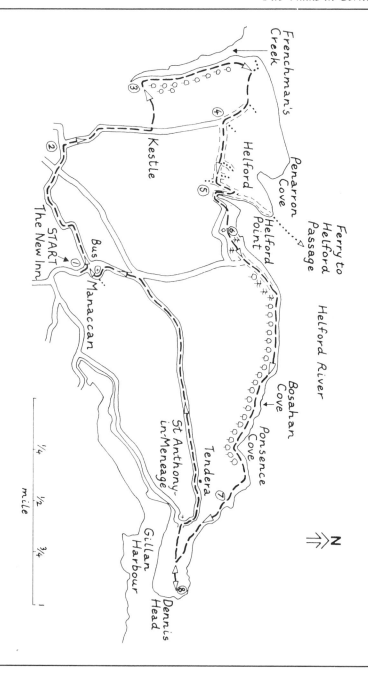

Bosahan Cove

3. Walk above the creek on your left along a shady woodland path. When this turns right, ascend steps and reach a partly-metalled lane. Turn right along it. Bear right at a fork. Pass a track leading down to Pengwedhen and Penarvon Cove on your left. Go ahead 30 yards.

4. Turn left down the partly-metalled track to Helford. Ignore two turnings on your left as you descend, before turning left with the lane which soon turns sharply right into Helford.

5. Turn left over the footbridge at the head of the inlet. Go left along a lane until it bends right. Fork left along the signposted Coast Path. Pass the entrance to the car park on your left and take a kissing gate with an acorn waymark ahead. Notice yachts in the River Helford over the hedge on your left.

6. A woodland path leads to a lane. Go right to a hairpin bend and leave the lane by taking the concessionary footpath through the Bosahan Estate ahead,. NO DOGS ARE ALLOWED HERE! Pass Bosahan and Ponsence Coves on your left. Eventually emerge through a kissing gate into a field.

7. Turn left to follow the hedge on your left. Continue over three stiles. After the fourth field, go ahead through a kissing gate. Reach a track leading from the end of this final field. Bear left over a waymarked stile to take the path to Dennis Head.

8. Return to the waymarked stile and go right to the final field again. Bear left and take a different kissing gate out of it, down a track to a road. Go right, soon passing a house called Tendera on your right. Go ahead along the road. Pass a signposted Public Footpath down to Helford on your right. Reach a crossroads and go left down to Manaccan. Divert left at the Den of Antiquity (now an antique and furniture shop, formerly a pub called 'The Cricketers') to visit the church. Continue downhill to the New Inn.

27. Lizard

Route: Lizard – Church Cove – Housel Cove – Lizard Point – Kynance Cove – Lizard.

Distance: 6¹/₂ miles.

Map: O.S. Pathfinder 1372 Lizard Point.

Start: The Top House, Lizard (Grid Reference SW703125).

Access: Lizard is the southernmost place in Britain, at the end of the A3083 from Helston. Cars can be parked near the Top House, while the No. 320 bus (weekday service from Truro via Helston) stops here.

The Top House (01326 290974)

Originally a farm building, this has been a pub since about 1790. It was called Hill's Hotel from the 1840s to the 1930s then Hill's Lizard Hotel. When Devenish Brewery bought it in 1951, they changed the name to the Lizard Hotel. The Hotel side of the business closed in 1986 and this became known as the Top House in contrast to another pub which used to exist lower down the village.

It is probably the only pub in the world with Serpentine beer pump handles. Real ale and bar meals are available. Children are welcome and there is a garden at the rear.

There is also a ghost, of a man called 'Boots', who died in the 1910s. He lived in the attic (the old staff room). He was last seen by Rita (who may be serving in the gift shop at Lizard Point) in January, 1991.

Opening hours are 11 am to 4 pm and 6 pm to 11 pm Mondays to Fridays, 11 am to 11 pm on Saturdays and noon to 3 pm and 7 pm to 10.30 pm on Sundays.

The Top House, Lizard

Lizard

The Lizard Peninsula stands strong and sombre in its age and isolation. Here is the old Serpentine rock that makes its geology unique. This is thought to be from the mantle between the earth's crust and core. It produces thin soils, rich in magnesium. Rare heathland plants grow on the poorly-drained plateau. The purplish stone is turned by craftsmen into attractive ornaments which can be bought locally. The veins running through it resemble the markings of a serpent, thus explaining the rock's name.

The Cornish language made its last stand here, with the last sermon in Cornish being preached in 1670 by the Rev. Francis Robinson in St. Winwallow's Church (the most southerly church in England). Lizard may be derived from 'Liazherd', a Cornish word for headland. Church Cove used to be busy with pilchard fishermen.

Now, the lifeboat is in neighbouring Kilcobben Cove. This is not the original Lizard lifeboat station, which was at Polpeor Cove and saved

562 lives between 1869 and 1961. An attempt was made to station a lifeboat here in 1885, but it was found too difficult to launch from. Eventually, a new station was built here to replace the old Lizard and Cadgwith lifeboats. The new boat saved 98 lives between 1961 and 1989. Some wrecks were caused by ships coming too close to the old Lloyd's signal station, which was located between Bass Point and the Lighthouse.

This lighthouse was built in 1751, although there was a predecessor (lit by candles) in the early 17th century. The present light has the power of several million candles and can be seen 20 miles out to sea. It would have been needed in 1720 when the military transport 'Royal Anne' was wrecked. 200 bodies were buried in a mass grave at Pistil Meadow. When you reach Kynance Cove, please refrain from trampling on the rare flora. The National Trust have provided a path down to the south-facing beach.

If you venture to the islands at low tide, remember to return before the water rises! There is wild asparagus on Asparagus Island. Prince Albert brought his children ashore here in 1846, while Tennyson paid his first visit two years later.

Kynance Cove

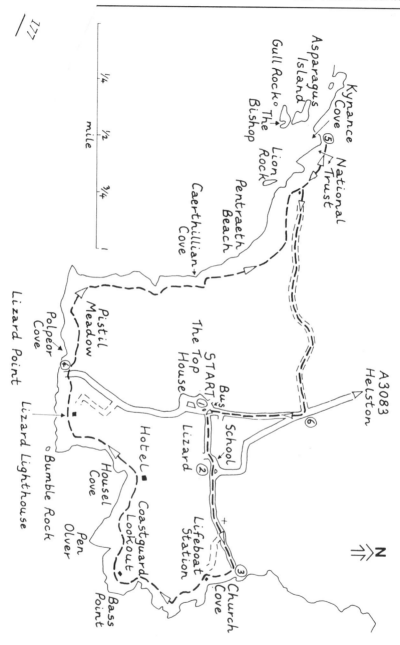

The Walk

1. Go ahead to the bus shelter and telephone box. Turn right along the road signposted as for the Lifeboat Station. Pass a general store on your right and a gift and craft shop on your left. Continue past a school on your left to reach a fork marked by an old stone cross.

2. Fork right along the road towards the Lifeboat Station. Pass St. Wynwallow's parish church of Landewednack on your left. Follow the road to its end at Church Cove.

3. Turn right with the Coast Path. Walk along the clifftops with the sea on your left. Pass the Lifeboat Station on your left, then Bass Point Coastguard Look-out on your right. Continue past Housel Bay Hotel on your right, above Housel Cove on your left. Pass Lizard Lighthouse on your right to reach the gift shop at Lizard Point (where Rita may be able to tell you about 'Boots', the ghost).

4. Continue along the Coast Path above the sea on your left. Pass Pistil Meadow on your right, then the Head on your left. Pass above Pentreath Beach on your left and enter National Trust land. Pass through the car park, with its toilet block and seasonal refreshments. Follow the path ahead down to Kynance Cove.

5. Retrace your steps up to the National Trust car park. Follow the access lane to the main road.

6. Turn right and very soon fork right to follow the road into Lizard. Pass the car park on your right. The Top House is ahead, on your right.

Land's End

Also of interest:

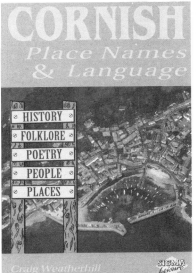

CORNISH PLACE NAMES & LANGUAGE

This unique book is written by Craig Weatherhill - historian, novelist and one of the few who are fluent in the Cornish language.

It includes the derivations of nearly 2,000 traditional Cornish place names plus snippets of history, folklore, local stories and poetry written in the ancient Cornish language. Dip into this book and a holiday in Cornwall takes on a whole new meaning!

£6.95

EXPLORE THE COAST OF DEVON

This is the complete coastal guide for walkers - but even motorists will find much to enjoy. It explores both the north and south coasts of Devon, following the entire 180 miles of the South West Coast Path that lie within Devon. Virtually every place of interest is included, plus tourist attractions, and stories about local characters, folklore and off-beat facts.

£6.95

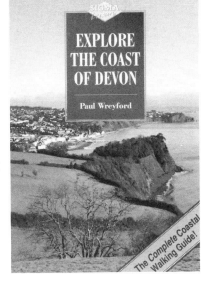

"Myths and Legends of Cornwall" is packed with folklore and factual stories that have fascinated visitors, scholars and local people for many years. The illustrations on these two pages are by the 19th century chronicler, J. T. Blight.

Far left: Boscawen stone crcle

Left: Land's End

Below: "Chair Ladder" – the "chair" at the top is where the legendary witch Madge Figgis sat to cast up storms. Also, where a mystery light has often been seen.

We also publish a super range of outdoor and local heritage books.:

South-West Walks

PUB WALKS *in*

SOUTH DEVON

Laurence Main

BEST PUB WALKS IN NORTH DEVON

PUB WALKS IN SOUTH DEVON

PUB WALKS ON DARTMOOR

TEA SHOP WALKS IN SOUTH DEVON

all £6.95 each

Round and about:

TEASHOP WALKS IN THE COTSWOLDS – Norman and June Buckley *(£6.95)*

IN SEARCH OF SWALLOWS AND AMAZONS: Arthur Ransome's Lakeland – Roger Wardale *(£6.95)*

100 LAKE DISTRICT HILL WALKS – Gordon Brown *(£7.95)*

LAKELAND ROCKY RAMBLES: Geology beneath your feet – Brian Lynas *(£9.95)*
(Companion Snowdonia volume, same author, same price, same high standards!)

PUB WALKS IN THE LAKE DISTRICT – Neil Coates *(£6.95)*

LAKELAND WALKING, ON THE LEVEL – Norman Buckley *(£6.95)*

– plus many more entertaining and educational books being regularly added to our list. All of our books are available from your local bookshop. In case of difficulty, or to obtain our complete catalogue, please contact:

Sigma Leisure, 1 South Oak Lane, Wilmslow, Cheshire SK9 6AR
Phone: 01625 – 531035   Fax: 01625 – 536800
E-mail: sigma.press@zetnet.co.uk

ACCESS and VISA orders welcome – call our friendly sales staff or use our 24 hour Answerphone service! Most orders are despatched on the day we receive your order – you could be enjoying our books in just a couple of days. Please add £2 p&p to all single copy orders. (Two or more, post free.)